BEYOND SURVIVING
A COMPILATION OF STORIES FROM
SURVIVORS OF SUICIDE LOSS

Edited By Jenni Klock Morel

All proceeds go to benefit
Survivors of Suicide Loss San Diego,
A Nonprofit Organization

This book is dedicated to everyone who has ever
lost a loved one to suicide.
It is our hope that within these stories you can find hope
and a little peace during your time of healing.

TABLE OF CONTENTS

INTRODUCTION
By Jenni Klock Morel

Welcome to beyond surviving, and I am sorry that you are here. I want to tell you that my heart breaks for your loss; but more importantly, I want to tell you that you are not alone.

This raw and beautiful anthology was born of a vision I had. At the time I had served on the Survivors of Suicide Loss San Diego (SOSL) Board of Directors for six-months, and had recently accepted a position as SOSL's Director of Development. I had this vision, sort of a lucid dream, of creating a collection of stories, mostly a compilation of articles previously published in the SOSL quarterly newsletters. I thought offering the wisdom of those many stories and articles in one place would benefit survivors, and have a worldwide reach. The book you are reading today is a much bigger embodiment of that original vision.

As I began the journey of collecting stories for this book, a snowball effect took hold, and more and more people stepped forward to share their stories. The outpouring of support for this project was overwhelming. Our contributing authors were grateful to be included, to have a chance to share their story in their own voice, and we were so grateful for their commitment to our organization, our cause, and our mission to help other survivors.

Some of the most difficult memories many of us share are our memories of when we first heard that our loved one died; and not only that they were gone, but that it was by suicide. Gone, forever—and we didn't get to say goodbye. Part I of this book shares personal stories of the initial shock that is a common theme for many of us.

After the initial shock, we had to figure out how to go on. Not to "move on," but how to carry on. How to keep on living. How to get out of bed and make it to work, or how to get the kids ready for school, or, even how to find the strength to take a shower. I think it is fair to say that many of us still struggle with some of these seemingly simple tasks. For some it remains a challenge on how to handle birthdays, anniversaries, holidays, and "Angel Days," as I like to call the date that our loved ones died. Part II of this book explores how survivors handled their grief after the initial shock wore off.

Finally, Part III of this book focuses on Hope. The title *Beyond Surviving* comes from this final part and our purpose we share with you: Hope. This includes the strength that we have found, the ways in which we have somehow managed to turn our grief and healing journey into something positive, and hope that all of us survivors, while we will never forget, and we will never "move on," we can move *forward*, and *live* once again.

SHARE WITH US

We invite you to share with us your reactions to the stories in this book. Please let us know what stories meant the most to you and how they affected you.

We also invite you to send us stories you would like to see published in either our quarterly newsletter "Hope & Comfort," on our webpage www.SOSLsd.org, or possibly, even in a 2nd edition of this very book.

Please send submissions to:
info@SOSLsd.org

or

SOSL
P.O. Box 3297
La Mesa, CA 91944

We hope you find as much healing and hope in this book as we did in compiling, editing, and writing it. It has truly been a tribute to those we have loved and lost.

Part I
Shock

"The soul would have no rainbow had the eyes no tears."
- John Vance Cheney

MAKING SENSE OF MY LOSS: LIFE WILL NEVER BE THE SAME

By Sarah M. Connelly

*The following is a lecture given at a church service in collaboration with my church minister. I asked if he would allow me to share my story in the hopes that it might help someone else.

March 18, 2005 started out to be the most wonderful day. At the time Chloe, my oldest daughter was five and her little sister, Ella, was six-months old. We were attending a Purim carnival at my daughter's preschool. The weather was perfect. A beautiful spring day. I remember standing on the lawn of the playground looking out at all the kids laughing and running around. I was thinking to myself: "What a wonderful moment. How lucky am I to have two wonderful kids, a great husband, everything in my life is great. I am so grateful." I had no idea that in the next few minutes my life would change forever.

I am a worrier so I always have my cell phone with me just in case something happens. On this day I was busy helping with the carnival and had left my phone in the stroller instead of with me in my pocket. I had picked it up earlier and noticed a few missed calls. I thought to myself I will check them as soon as I get Ella to sleep. So there I was standing there rocking my six-month old to sleep, thinking how grateful I am, then my phone rang. It was my younger sister. I knew right away from the sound of her voice something was wrong. I assumed she was upset about a boyfriend or that our mom had done something to upset her.

"Amanda, what's wrong?" She said nothing. I could hear her crying, sobbing the out-of-breath type of crying. She could barely whisper the words.... "It's Dylan."

I asked where he was, what happened. My thought was that he had picked a fight with the wrong person and was in the hospital. Before I could say anything she said, "he's dead." My knees gave out and I fell to the ground with Ella in my arms. I started screaming "NO, NO, NO" over and over and I remember thinking "this is not happening." Some other moms came over and helped me up. One mom took Ella and someone else was trying to reassure the other kids that everything was OK. They took me inside and I remember sitting there thinking "this isn't happening." I remember talking but I don't remember what I said. Someone called my husband and they told him to come to the school. We got things situated and left to be with my family.

That was almost two years ago. Some days it feels like it happened yesterday. I was 30 years old and my brother was 27. He would have turned 28 that June. I have three brothers and one sister. I am the oldest. I was the typical big sister, bossy and protective. We lived in a very chaotic house with very dysfunctional parents. I took on the role of protector, guardian and parent. Whenever I think of my childhood, I think about my twin brothers Dylan and Ryan. It is as if there is no separation. In my mind it was always me and my brothers. We were always together when we were younger. We played and fought just like siblings do. But I took my role as protector very seriously. It wasn't until Dylan died that I realized how much I worried about him. When he died it forced me to look at how we grew up and how hard it was for all of us. I tried so hard to take care of my siblings. So when Dylan died, I blamed myself. I still do. I don't think I will ever completely be rid of the guilt. I blamed myself for not being a better sister. I blamed myself for trying to get out of our chaotic house and leaving my siblings behind.

Dylan and I drifted apart the older we got. There was this weird awkwardness between us. But at the same time whenever he saw me he gave the best hugs. The last time I saw him was about a year before he died. We were at our sister's high school graduation. I hadn't seen him in a while. I was mad at him but I never told him that. He was still using drugs and I just found out his new girlfriend was pregnant. I thought he was being irresponsible. I just wanted him to get clean and get his life together. I was tired of seeing him so miserable. I found him in this big crowd of people. He didn't say anything to me. He just came up to me and hugged me so tight. We stood there hugging for at least 5 minutes. He was crying and had his head buried in my shoulder. He never said a word. But I kept saying, "It's okay. I am here for you."

My sister was standing there watching and I could see the tears running down her cheeks. He finally let go and I said, "Please call me." He never called. The last time he called was to tell me that his girlfriend had given birth to a little boy. His little boy was nine—months old when he died. My brother also left behind two other kids —another son and a daughter.

Dylan's life was so complicated. Around the age of 14 he started using drugs. The drugs eventually took over his life. He tried to quit so many times. Everyone knows that most people turn to drugs as a way to cope with stuff they can't handle. That was Dylan. There were five of us all together growing up with two abusive parents. While we all got our fair share of abuse, Dylan had it the worst. It was his personality that made him an easy target. The rest of us learned to keep our mouths shut, but Dylan never did. He was impulsive and couldn't just stand by and let someone belittle him or abuse him. He never understood why his mom didn't love him. At his memorial I talked about how Dylan was far too sensitive to live in this world with so many cruelties.

He couldn't shrug things off. If someone said something mean to him he took it inside and felt it deeply. He would give anyone the shirt off his back and would stand up to anyone who said something mean about his big sister. I think he started doing drugs to bury the pain and then it didn't take long for him to become an addict.

I wasn't around the night my brother died. I was living about two hours away from him. I had my own life and tried not to look back that often. I always thought that there would be time. I always had hope that Dylan would get clean and then we would reconnect. My other siblings talked to Dylan the night he died. His girlfriend had kicked him out of their house a few weeks earlier. She said she couldn't have an addict around the baby. I don't know why this night was any different but on March 17, 2005, Dylan got drunk and high and starting calling his girlfriend asking to please let him come back home. She told him "No, not until you are clean." So Dylan started calling my siblings and asking them to call his girlfriend and convince her. They called her but they agreed with her that he needed to get clean. I don't know what happened but Dylan started threatening suicide. My brother and sister called the police but they never responded. I didn't hear any of this until after Dylan had died. My brother and sister blame themselves for not taking his threat more seriously. He had made threats like this before. But he usually slept it off. No one knows why this night was different. He was staying with a friend and at some point during the night put a rope around his neck and hung himself.

While making the arrangements for Dylan's memorial I asked to be with him. I sat in the room with his cold body underneath an orange polyester blanket, sobbing and apologizing to him over and over. "I am so sorry I let you down. I am so sorry I wasn't here. I am so sorry I didn't help you." I will never forget being in that room with his body, knowing that he was gone but not really believing it. I wanted so badly to grab him and hug him and make everything okay. It took me about six-months to realize he was really gone. After I got home from the memorial, I still found myself worrying about him. It wasn't until he was gone that I realized how much I thought about him. Even though we rarely saw each other, he was in my thoughts every day. Every time I saw a handsome young man on a motorcycle I thought of him. Every time I saw a blond man in a black leather jacket I thought of him. During those first few months I would try to convince myself that it was all a mistake, a bad dream. I would have dreams about saving him, that I had reached him in time and I saved him. I would look for him wherever I went. Grief does weird things to your mind. The pain of losing someone, who has always been a part of your life and who is a part of you, is so great that I think sometimes your mind can't deal with it and tries to cope anyway it knows how.

In March *(2007)*, it will be the two year anniversary of his death. Dylan's death made me become a part of a group that I never wanted to be a part of. Without my consent I became a survivor of suicide loss. I am still learning what it means to be a part of this group. The journey of a survivor can go in many different directions. For me, my journey has to include education and understanding. Educating myself, educating others and trying to understand something that at many times makes no sense. I am now obligated to share Dylan's story. This topic and my story may force people outside of their emotional safety zone. However, when people go outside of their safety zone, that is when real progress or awareness is made.

Dylan's story and my story are not unique. How many kids today are growing up in abusive houses? How many of those kids slip through the cracks? How many people seek treatment for depression or addiction only to find that their insurance, if they have any, doesn't cover that kind of treatment? How many kids do we know that just don't fit the mold of our traditional educational system? Do you know anyone like Dylan who is artistic, impulsive and sensitive? Dylan loved to live on the edge. As a child he would climb to the top of any jungle gym and never think twice. He would jump into the pool before he knew how to swim, and he drove fast where ever he went, and the music always had to be as loud as it could go.

There are many issues involved when someone takes their own

life. More than 90% of people who die by suicide have a diagnosable mental disorder, and depression is more common than any other disorder. Is our health care system and our society doing all they can to make people aware of the symptoms of depression? Do we teach our youth that it is okay to feel sad and that it is okay to ask for help? Dylan didn't take his life because he was selfish or weak. Like most people who take their own life, he just wanted the pain to end.

Dylan often confided in his twin brother that he felt like the black sheep of the family. He felt like he was letting us all down. He felt like he was letting his kids down. For someone as sensitive as he was, it was too much to handle. He tried many times to get sober but it never lasted. Each time he relapsed he felt worse about himself. In those final moments, the pain was too much. He was too tired.

We have to talk about the subject of depression and suicide. Talking about it doesn't make it happen. I have never been ashamed of my brother. Just like I would never be ashamed of someone who had diabetes or cancer. My brother had an illness. I actually had someone at his memorial give me their condolences, but not because I lost my brother but because it was so sad that Dylan was going to a different place than I was. Many of my friends and family don't ask about Dylan or how I am doing. There is a stigma around suicide. People are afraid to talk about it. Part of that stigma might exist because of our need to try and make sense of everything. Suicide doesn't make sense to those of us who are not in that kind of pain. But to that person who is suffering, in that moment, they cannot see a way out.

So… my mission now is to be a person who stands up and lets people know that we need to talk about depression and suicide. There is nothing I can do to bring my brother back, but there are so many things I would have done differently if I would have known. Dylan had almost every single risk factor for suicide: history of mental disorders, history of alcohol and substance abuse, family history of suicide, family history of childhood maltreatment, feelings of hopelessness, impulsive or aggressive tendencies, barriers to accessing mental health treatment, loss (relational, social, work, or financial), physical illness, easy access to lethal methods, unwillingness to seek help because of the stigma attached to mental health and substance abuse disorders or suicidal thoughts, and isolation, and a feeling of being cut off from other people.

Even after spending four-years in high school, four-years in college and two-years in graduate school, I didn't know that my own brother was at risk. By sharing Dylan's story I hope that it brings some awareness to people. By sharing his story I give his death some sort of meaning where there was none.

Author's Note: In closing, I would just like to say "thank you" to Fresno Survivors of Suicide Loss. We are lucky that there is such a great organization in Fresno. They not only help survivors after the death of a loved one but they speak to over 6,000 individuals a year, half of those are youth in the classroom settings. I would also like to thank Bryan Jessup for working with me on this and for everyone here for listening.

Surviving: A Parent's Story
By Mike Turner

There was a knock on the door at 5 a.m.

"Mr. Turner, I am a county officer. I need to talk with you." I told him to wait while I quickly got dressed.

"What is it?" my wife asked.

"Nothing good," I answered, fearing that my 17-year-old son Jeremy had been in a car accident. He had just bought his first car. When I invited the officer in, he informed me that he was with the Medical Examiner's Office. My son, Jeremy, had taken his life by shooting himself with a shotgun in a Chula Vista parking lot. Several of his friends had witnessed it.

It was as if lightning had hit the room. Like a concussion of thunder; the silence knocked me to the floor. The unimaginable had happened. Our lives have never been the same since.

Jeremy was an only child. Three years prior, he found his mother dead in her bed from a heart attack. He never allowed himself to grieve. After I remarried, things seemed normal until a couple of months prior to his death. He started to dress in punk attire. He fell in love with a girl who was a year older and lived on her own. When he learned that she didn't feel for him the same way he did for her, he acquired a gun without our knowledge. We believe he must have planned a dramatic exit in the parking lot of the restaurant where she worked.

Jeremy's mother had symptoms of schizophrenia before she died. As I pieced things together later, I learned from his friends that he lived in a much different world than he showed at home. In retrospect, I think Jeremy inherited tendencies that were starting to engulf him. Like an avalanche, his mental state overwhelmed him very quickly. In the summer before his death, he seemed like a normal adolescent. But within six weeks, he changed dramatically. The more we became concerned, the more he refused to get counseling. We never dreamed it would come to suicide. It happened so fast.

As a parent, suicide seems like the ultimate failure. My best was not good enough to help him. There are so many "should haves" that buffeted me with guilt and frustration. The deep visceral ache seemed more painfully real than a broken bone. It was very uncomfortable to share this tragedy with other people who felt sorry but did not really understand.

Sharing one's feelings with people who understand can be very healing. It is a process. Time does not heal on its own, but it does take time to heal. As survivors, we can never be the same, but we can find healing and eventual relief, especially if we can share our hurt with others who understand. This is the reason for SOSL - to provide a place of healing for those who have experienced this tragedy.

I Didn't Want to Write This
By Danny's Mom

"For my precious and beloved son, Daniel."
May 8, 1980 - July 27, 2007

I didn't want to write this.

I said I didn't want to have to keep hearing my son Danny tell me how unhappy and frustrated he was in his marriage. Now I never hear from Danny at all.

This isn't what I had in mind, God.

I said I wanted a dog exactly like Danny's. I said I needed an incentive to get daily exercise. Now I have Danny's dog, and I walk him at least twice a day, rain or shine, dark or light.

This isn't what I had in mind, God.

I said I wanted to meet new people. Decent people—people I could relate to. Now I meet compassionate, intelligent, caring people once a month. We call ourselves Survivors of Suicide Loss.

This isn't what I had in mind, God.

This isn't at all what I had in mind.

SHOCK

By Tiffany B. "33"

Shock. That's the best word I can use to describe my initial reaction to finding out my brother killed himself. Utter shock. To say I was surprised would be an understatement. My brother was my best friend. We knew each other inside and out. So I thought. He was the only person in this world who truly knew me from childhood. We took care of each other. We raised each other. He knew my feelings, what I was thinking before I said it, and often finished my sentences. We laughed at the same jokes, cried at the same sad stories, liked the same music (sometimes), and went to concerts together. People often thought we were twins, but at 33, he was three years younger than I was. But when he told me he was addicted to heroin, it was the first time I didn't know who he was.

His struggle with this ugly drug is not something I would've expected. Yes, he did the recreational experimenting, smoked, drank, but never in a million years, would I ever think he'd touch that stuff! Until the day he said his ex-girlfriend was the one who stuck the needle in his arm.

Not too long after he divulged this information to me, he was on and off again with this girlfriend. Then the depression began. They soon broke up, he moved out, and this is when I started to notice odd changes in him. He said he was sober, however, I said he wasn't to come over to our house, and be around my kids if he was ever using. He didn't come around as often. My kids were questioning, "Why isn't Uncle coming over; Where is Uncle?" He had to move in with our mother, which to say the least, wasn't the best option for him. He then swore he was sober-and was at our house all the time! We loved this guy! He was joyful, had a good job, played and loved his nieces, and enjoyed our family time! However, he still had no money... we couldn't figure out why. He was living rent free, ate meals at our house and hardly went out in the evenings, so where was his money going???

I remembered that story about the woman in Coronado, who had hung herself (allegedly) after her step son died. My brother was SO intrigued by how it happened, what she used, and all the logistics. Also, the Real Housewives of Beverly Hills husband who hung himself...he was very interested in that story too. But at the time, when we talked about it, nothing seemed abnormal to me. We often discussed news, daily interests, etc. Matter of fact, he always thought I was the gruesome one, since I was always into the "gory details." In hindsight, I guess it was all mental notes for him.

There wasn't a day that went by, when my brother didn't call me. Even if he didn't want to chat, he would at least text me, or tell me flat out that he didn't want to talk. So, the weekend of November 18th was when I started to worry, when he wasn't returning my phone calls...

It was Friday, the 18th of November, when my brother was supposed to come over and hang out with us. He said he was getting off of work and going over to our grandmother's house to wish her a Happy Birthday. He said he would call afterwards, and make plans from there. I never heard back from him that evening. Saturday morning, when I spoke to him, he said he would be over to watch the Charger game with us later that evening. I thought I'd take a quick nap to prep for the night. Wish I'd known that was the last time I'd ever speak to him again. He called and texted me while I was napping, asking me if I could chat for a minute. When I woke up 30-

minutes after that text and voicemail, I tried calling him back, but he was already gone.

By Sunday night, our mother thought it would be a good idea to file a missing persons report. So, I met her at her house, and the police took our information, and said there wasn't much we could do since he wasn't a threat to society, didn't have a record, or wasn't under a doctor's care. We called every hospital and jail in San Diego and nothing. Come Monday morning I received the call from our mother that the Mexican Consulate called to tell her they found my brother-dead.

That was when my world stopped. Immediately, I was in disbelief. I needed to see him in order to believe it. I remember having my husband driving me to my mother's house, while I was looking for his car parked along the street. I couldn't believe it. My best friend, brother, children's uncle, was gone.

My immediate reaction was disbelief, then absolute sadness, then anger. I was MAD at him for leaving our family, leaving my children, and for leaving ME. I wanted to punch somebody! How could he do this to me!!?? Later, I realized, it's not about me. It's about him, and what made him happy—and allowed him to not be in pain anymore.

As it turns out, my brother drove to Rosarito, Mexico, Saturday afternoon immediately after calling/texting me. He checked himself into a hotel down there, possibly played golf, bought some beers, some heroin, shot up, wrote a note, and hung himself on Sunday.

I couldn't get down to Mexico fast enough! I *had* to see him with my own eyes in order to believe he was dead. The drive down to Mexico was the longest drive of my life. After the difficult conversations with the morgue, and funeral home, trying to find their location was even harder. It was like some hole in the wall, with a garage attached to it. I knew going there that I would be the one to identify his body. I knew he would want me to be the one to do it too. Being led down a dark hallway into a garage with a hearse parked in it and a coffin next to that wasn't exactly setting the tone for me. Then, seeing the viewing window where his body was, took my breath away. His body was completely covered up all the way to his throat. He looked like he was asleep, totally at peace. I only wish that I didn't freak out as badly as I did. Looking back, I wish I'd stayed there in front of him, talking to him. Telling him how much I loved him, and how I hope he has found his peace.

After the logistics were taken care of, we had to find his car, wait for the "attorney" to help us with getting his belongings, give our statements to the police, and make the arrangements to come back down at another time, only to pick up his ashes to take them back across the border. The attorney and the police said that my brother left a note. I then didn't care about anything else but getting that note. I had to see what he said, what his last feelings were, what was going on in his head. I was anxious to know what he had with him, what belongings he left behind for us to collect. That part was wearing on me. I needed his "stuff." I'm not sure why I needed it so badly, almost as if I had his "stuff," I could make sense of it, or I could hold on longer…I still don't know…

A few days passed, and we had to return to Mexico in order to bring my brother back across the border into the US. We were anxious because we had his memorial service planned, and wanted to have his ashes with us for that. Additionally, we were to pick up his "stuff" as well. But in order to get his things, we had to be questioned longer, and more in depth, which in fact I believe was just a stall tactic for them to collect his belongings and go through and pillage the items they wanted to keep. There were items in the report missing from the items they provided to us. I couldn't get past the anger I felt towards these people! It was as if we owed them something for having my brother die in their country!!! So, we got the note, his backpack with his clothes, shoes, passport, and some other miscellaneous items. The note was more or less an apology to our mother, that he had a relapse with his heroin. It wasn't so much a goodbye note, or an explanation (which is what I was hoping for). My husband had to drive my brother's car, which was covered in crime scene dust, crime scene tape on every door, oh, and with his ashes in the back, across the border. I drove my car with his backpack, and other belongings. Come to find out that he still had some drug remnants in the backpack! We are so lucky we didn't get stopped by the border patrol!

With the memorial service coming up, I had in mind that I wanted to speak about my brother, like a eulogy of sorts. I thought about it up until the last minute, finally deciding that I just couldn't do it. I couldn't get up there and explain how I missed him, how I remembered him; how his death had affected me - it all seemed so unimportant at the time. I thought that nobody wanted to hear my side- especially when everyone was more concerned with how our mother was feeling, or coping, or doing. Nobody really asked how I was doing. I was more than willing to make all of the arrangements for my brother's memorial service. Having to get my brother's affairs in order, my emotions took a back seat. I don't think people understand what it is like to lose a sibling. Often, they are your closest relative, your longest friendship, and your tightest bond in the family. I think I was more frustrated than anything. But at the same time, it kind of put my feelings into perspective. I think that's what suicide does. It makes you put your feelings aside, because after all, it is about the one who just died, right?

Shortly after my brother's death, I went to a lot of group therapy meetings, as well as one on one therapy. I can honestly say that if it wasn't for these meetings, I am not sure how I could have coped. Talking about what happened, and about my personal experiences, really made me see that maybe my brother was actually very courageous for what he did. Not a lot of people will agree with me on this, but in due time, you may, one day...

It was not until after we brought my brother's car back across to the US, and went through the contents inside it, that we found out what kind of trouble he was in. We found so many of those money loan receipts, from so many locations, up to four a week! We found out he owed money on his taxes, had no money in his bank accounts, and had been using heroin for some time. No wonder he never had any money! He even wrote a list of people who he might have wanted to say his goodbyes to.

I read some of his emails, journals, notes to girlfriends, and realized just how tormented he really was, and he didn't ever share that side of himself with us. I always knew he had a dark side, but never would I have thought he'd kill himself, at least not intentionally. This is how I can explain why I think he was courageous for what he did. He knew he was trapped. He had demons in his head, he had to get out. To him, believing that this was his only option, and knowing he could not go on, I get it. He did not want to be a burden on anyone, didn't want to rely on anyone anymore. He didn't want to fight. In his mind, he had fought enough in his life. So this is why I understand it. It does not mean I condone suicide, or that I don't see that you can find a way to fix things, but I get HIM.

I have dealt with a lot of death in my lifetime. But I can honestly say that nothing compares to the loss due to suicide. You are left with so many questions, the why's, the how's, the "if only I'd," and of course, what could I have done to prevent this? Nothing prepares you for the shock, the loss, the details, and the guilt you have afterwards. I have done a lot of research, not only on my brother and his situation, but on suicide itself. Regardless of the situation, the story, there is always one common bond, and that is that a person you love dearly, has taken their own life, without warning, and the survivors are left with constant wonder, grief and loss.

Here I am a year later, and I am no longer looking under bridges or in trees, thinking I will see people hanging there. I have overcome this feeling through intensive therapy, group meetings and many books on suicide. I am however, still waiting for my brother to walk through my front door, as if he's been on a long trip to Thailand, or China. I know he's physically gone, but he is always in my heart, and on my mind, and sometimes in spirit and in my dreams!

All my love, forever and always,
Tiffany B. "33"

THE NEW "NORMAL" HAPPENED SO FAST.

By Christine Bruneau

The new "normal" happened so fast.
What's new is new and, just as fast - the past has passed.

The adjustments are thrown at everyone, before they even come into view.

Sometimes I bring your name up—just to keep you alive, as others look at me nodding, not knowing what to say.

I'm not as the others, who have not had this pain.

In one instant, the others and I are separated and understanding comfort, I cannot gain.

Each of us who lost you, unique sorrow, known only to them— how they will face tomorrow?

Then comes the part of looking at the ones left here.

Are they OK—could they do the same?

Will they feel your loss and choose the same *"Waiter, check please. I'm done."*

As a person who wants to "fix everything" and make it better, I admit to myself that it will never be better. It will just be the new "normal."

It takes time—we are all in personal stages of grief.

For Michael, our sorrow comes at the price of his relief.

Sometimes I feel sad when I realize it's been awhile since I thought about you. I haven't forgotten you.

Then out of nowhere, I can hear your laugh, see your smile and hear you singing - like you had never left.

Those are my reminders that you are at peace.

I will never forget you Michael—we aren't that far apart.

I miss you dearly but you are as close as my heart.

You confided in me that you knelt, with tears and prayed.

I find comfort in knowing that you told God how you felt.

Thanks for sharing a part of you with me. ~ mum

In Loving Memory, Michael, January 25th, 2013

MICHAEL STIMPSON:
1977-2013.

By Karen Cardon

T he last time I talked with Michael was in December 2012. He told me "I feel like a new man, Mom. I'm so happy that I've been going around the house singing." He said that he had a nervous breakdown and had been in the hospital for a few days. He had realized that he was an alcoholic and had quit drinking. It made me very happy. Afterwards I smiled as I thought about the way he always made people laugh and his contagious smile. It was my very best Christmas present.

When the phone call came from Tiffany telling me what had happened, I just knew there had been some kind of mistake. He loved his family more than anything in the world. When I realized that what she was saying was true, I was so shocked I felt like I was going crazy. Even as we planned the memorials we would be having for him, I just felt numb and nothing seemed real. I knew that Michael had a really hard time after his father died in 2010, but had no idea he had been so depressed for so long and was in so much pain.

On February 10th I wrote the following in my journal. "This will be the hardest entry that I will ever have to write. My beautiful, precious son, Michael, committed suicide on January 25th." I decided to go up to the cabin and get away from it all for a few days. It was there that I told Michael out loud about the agony I was feeling. I was so mad at him! I asked myself why again and again knowing there wasn't an answer. Most of all I cried and told him how much I missed him. Death never comes at the right time but especially when it's death by suicide.

I thought about what my friend Deanna said in one of her songs, "If we could take the sorrow out of every loss that comes along, we'd have to take the loving out of life." This terrible sorrow, this hole in my heart, is happening because I loved him so much. Sometime later I received a book from Christal's mother (Michael's mother-in-law) entitled, "Dying To Be Free." Bless her for sensing what I needed. I found out that a suicide happens every 17 minutes in the United States; the majority occurring with young people. I realized that the emotional roller coaster I had been going through was normal and that I wasn't really going crazy. It seems even more important in the world today that we talk openly about suicide with our children, family and friends. It's the hidden secret that no one talks about.

When I came to the section about those of us referred to as survivors, I thought how it would make me feel if I was the mother who went to check on her son when she didn't hear his music and discovered that he had hung himself in his room. I realized then how lucky we were that we didn't have to go through that kind of memory for the rest of our lives. I felt a sweet peaceful feeling come over me at that moment and felt like he was telling me it would be okay. I am so grateful for the knowledge I have of a loving God who is taking care of Michael until the day that we can be together again. I'm glad that he is at peace and free from the pain that took his life. In the end we realize that it's all about letting go.

"What the caterpillar calls the end of the world, the master calls a butterfly."—Richard Bach

A MOTHER'S ACCOUNT OF HER DAUGHTER'S LIFE

By Mary W.

Sharon was always the happy child, loving life. She excelled in school and was an honor student and yes, she did the normal naughty things most teens do. During her senior year she did half of her day at a local high school and attended a community college the second half of the day. While growing up she was a girl scout, played soccer, volleyball and was on the swim team during high school. In middle school she was involved in school politics. Everyone thought she was happy, healthy and well adjusted.

After graduating from high school she went to college and moved out of the family home. After a couple of years she dropped out of school and went to work full time. Her decline began with partying and drugs. Finally she became disenchanted with that lifestyle and moved back home, only to discover she was pregnant. Coming to the realization that she had to clean up her life, she entered school again and gave birth to her son. At this point she appeared healthy and happy. After finishing a community college, she entered San Diego State's nursing program and graduated with a BS degree in nursing. Also while in nursing school she met a man she fell in love with.

Shortly after graduation she was hired as a surgical ICU nurse and had a wonderful career. Sharon and the love of her life bought a house and blended their family together. Her partner had a son and so did she. Two years later her partner wanted to move to Texas where the housing market was very lucrative. The agreement was that if Sharon wanted to move back close to her family they would after a year. So they sold their house and moved.

After a year, Sharon was extremely depressed because she missed her family. Her partner had purchased a few properties including a beautiful new home they lived in and refused to move back. All of their money was tied up and Sharon was unable to move back, thus the depression increased. She entered treatment which consisted of anti-depressants and therapy. Nothing helped. In fact, it made the problem worse. Finally she and her partner moved back home and she seemed to improve.

Again they bought a house. Sharon's partner decided he wanted to go into business with his friend in Arizona and she refused to move. Her love went into business and left her here. For a while she seemed okay with the arrangement. After a few months she started to steal drugs from work and was fired and was going to lose her nursing license. One of the stipulations from the nursing board was she had to go into rehab, and she did and was well on her road to recovery. Her partner decided he wouldn't participate with her recovery because he, being a nurse, knew everything he needed to know about addiction and depression. This was like a slap in the face to her. Then disaster struck again. Her father was diagnosed with a brain tumor and was operated on, leaving him paralyzed.

While she was recovering from the shock of her father's condition, she was notified that charges were being brought against her for stealing drugs at the hospital where she worked. She left rehab a week later to face the charges and was put on probation. Even though this was a tremendous blow to her pride, she was still on the road to recovery. When her father came home she nursed him. He was told he'd never even stand for any length of time, but Sharon had him taking a few steps, feeding himself and doing many things the doctors thought he wouldn't be able to do. Again she seemed happy and healthy.

Then her partner decided he wasn't going to enable her anymore and permanently left her. She began to slip again into a deep depression. Because of her criminal record, she could not get a job, bills were not paid, and she could not take care of her 16-year old son's basic needs.

At 37-years-old, on October 11, 2011 Sharon died by suicide. She was a registered nurse, well educated, a mother with a 16-year old son, and she was seriously depressed.

This is written by a mother who greatly misses a wonderful daughter who was seriously depressed. The drugs were her way of escape from being lonely and unhappy. If you knew her you would have thought she was fine, until her final day she tried to be strong not letting anyone know the torment she was under. The pieces to her puzzle were not known until after her death. Unfortunately her partner and the love of her life kept many secrets from her family. RIP, my baby girl!

HE JUST COULDN'T HOLD ON ANYMORE.

By Regina Hawkins

There were signs.

I didn't really need any, I had always known.

I was just waiting. Waiting for the phone call.

One day he was wearing a cheap gold chain, like super thick and cheap, from some sort of quarter toy machine for adults going through a later mid-life crisis, baby boomer bling. Then he gave me his Bose iPod dock, he loved it but his iPod had just been stolen and he apparently had no intentions of replacing it. I carried it home like a dead cat with a diamond collar, I wanted it but I knew it would always stink. He came by on Christmas morning, rushed, he told me he almost left my gift on the porch when I didn't answer the door quickly enough. He hugged me like it was the last hug he would ever give me and told me he loved me. And he was gone.

I had been waiting for this moment for years, since before I was ever born. My life up until the phone call was merely a series of events leading up to the moment that my heart would be shattered irreparably.

"Your Father, your Father......."

"My Father what!"

" .... "

"F-----g say it!"

"Your Father committed suicide."

A scream came from me that was like no other sound I had ever heard, guttural moans emanated like fire from my throat and into the depths of the pillow I smashed my face into. I didn't know what else to do but to continually scream "f---" for minutes, until my throat was hoarse and I could yell no more. I was breaking, completely, my brain, my heart, and my soul. It was all crumbling to pieces, a jumbled mess of undefinable pain.

As I calmed, exhausted of tears, of screams, I attempted to breathe, hiccuping gasps of still night air. And then I felt it, a tiny bit of relief, the waiting was over. I hated myself so much for that, I still do.

The waiting had almost done me in as well. The weeks leading up to his suicide were a chaotic series of drunken nights and lost meandering days disrupted only by the click of my lighter and the occasional manic outburst which others tried so very hard to ignore. I was his misunderstood distress beacon. Even when I plainly stated to other family members, "He is going to kill himself," it was as if I were the crazy one, as if I was the one who needed help. Well, I did need help. I needed my Father. And I saw him, felt him disappearing at a rate I was not prepared for, could never prepare myself for. I felt myself being sucked down with him. I knew I couldn't save him but maybe if I tried hard enough I could at least feel what he was feeling, as if my empathy could manifest into an actual state of existence and go with him, wherever he felt compelled to go.

After.....yeah, that's it. Everything has become before and after. How a late afternoon walk in the grass used to be just a regular lazy day thing to do suddenly feels like a bittersweet memory, a hazy dream with sticky feet and a heavy heart, an undeserved gift. I was dumb, naive as to what real pain could feel like. I dealt with this enormous blow by first taking my soul and lighting fire to it then quickly wrapping it up very tightly so as to cut off any oxygen, yes souls need oxygen too. Numbness, I fell into it completely, my eyes stared blankly as I lit cigarette after cigarette as if it were the only thing reminding me to breathe. In and out, lungs doing their thing, blood circulating because it has a direction, a purpose. What now? What was I supposed to do? I could hide. Yes, why not? I could just crawl into bed and disappear. Everyone would understand. Hushed tones outside my bedroom door, "Poor thing, she loved her Daddy so." People could bring me tea and sandwiches and encourage me to eat. I imagined myself not bathing for weeks and then finally taking a hot bubble bath, emerging a glowing refreshed version of myself. And then of course I remember that I am the one that holds s--t together, I am the one who takes care of people, aside from my Father of course.

He was the favorite, always had been. He was the youngest of 8 children and a show off from the start. He grew to a full 6 feet 4 inches of handsome gentleman; a charismatic storyteller, a smooth talking ladies' man, a trouble maker of the endearing variety, a genuine friend, a caring Father, Uncle and Grandfather. He was always just a phone call away with whatever was needed, no questions asked. He carried himself in such a way that just made you want to be near him. There was never an empty chair at his side, in fact you had to move quick to claim the coveted seat next to his. He held the family together, I mean when it came to laying down the law he really took special care in making sure everyone heard it and understood it. He often made his point be known by taking his index finger and bluntly poking the table until one day he poked the damn thing broken. I personally got a kick out of that one. He struggled for days with his swollen finger insisting it was fine until he finally gave in and applied a popsicle stick splint. For some reason the thud of his left index finger hitting the wooden table just didn't feel quite as authoritative.

I took after my Father, I convinced people that my way was best in such a charming fashion that they had no idea I was manipulating them. Pops taught me good. I watched him work his magic and learned that a sincere smile and a firm handshake or a close embrace could get just about anyone to trust you. He made a damn good Salesman. I became a Barista and worked my charms behind the espresso bar while yearning for so much more in life yet inexorably drawn to the bean. For years I worked at a drive thru espresso bar that was on his way home from work. He stopped in every afternoon for a pick me up. He left a hefty tip whether I was on shift or not. Occasionally he also needed a place to dispose of his empties so my Mother wouldn't find them in the trash at home. He thought he was so crafty with his discovery of the extra long Slurpee straw. He could put a forty between his legs with one of those long straws and drink hands free (and inconspicuously as well). Oh, had I failed to mention his vices? That list just might be as long as the list of his more appealing (however maybe not as fun) attributes. Getting drunk with Dad, that was a blast and a half. I have never more enjoyed a night of intoxication as much as I did with my Father. We shared many bottles, laughs and smokes. However we both shared more than our healthy share of the first and the latter by ourselves. We both secretly (or maybe it wasn't such a secret) fell deeper and deeper into the bottle, occasionally coming up for air long enough to make sure the facade was intact, that the paint hadn't chipped away too badly, that the foundation wasn't crumbling completely, then back down we went.

He kept going, f--k *appearances, let it all hang out.*

I, however, figured out how to manage appearances and a s--t load of other problems while sprawled at the bottom of the bottle. Maybe I found a peep hole, a secret window that all alcoholics come across if they live long enough. Watch me function, I dare you. I was on a mission now. I had never been "weak" and I wasn't about to start now. *F--k it. I'm in charge now.*

I was drowning in the details, I didn't dare look at the big picture, not yet. There were phone calls to be made, like a million phone calls. He left instructions, all the important information; what bills had been paid, what bills should be paid soon, bank account numbers, passwords, insurance information and a stack of credit cards and such next to a glass still smelling faintly of gin. I quickly poured myself a few fingers and lit a cigarette. I clicked on his computer and got to work.

Another aspect of his life that I acquired was my Mother.

The last thing in the world that I ever imagined myself doing was to put my Mother to bed on my couch complete with a kiss on the forehead. That is not the sort of relationship we had, very far from it. In fact, I can't even remember how many invitations I declined over the years because I was so put off by the idea of spending any time with her at all.

Their relationship was like a long drawn out dog fight. At times, it was a full on battle, other times they just circled each other, silently waiting for the first lunge. After, they would lick their wounds and commence appearances. It took over 30 years for one of them to finally let go.

I cooked my Mother's meals, which she picked at fretfully. I poured myself wine and looked at food as if it were a foreign concept, wondering how I ever put such strange solid items in my mouth. I felt as if showering were a necessary chore that took way too much time. I might miss something. I had to be available at all times to everyone and for any request. Sleep came in short gasps, waking sweaty, eyes wide and muscles stiff. The knot that took the place in my body where my stomach once was grew tighter by the hour.

My Mother became unpredictable, at times almost infantile. She asked for crayons, stating that she would like to color. I got her a pack of crayons and made phone calls while she doodled blue daisies on the back of a Pennysaver.

At midnight on December 31, 2008, three days after my Father died by suicide, she decided to run out in the street with a pot and a big wooden spoon. Banging wildly she screamed, "Happy f-----g New Year, WOOOOOOO!"

My very generous and always helpful Mother-in-law took her grocery shopping about a week after. I was grateful for the reprieve which I spent the same way I spent every free moment that week, on the phone. They returned about an hour later. My Mother got out of the car stone faced and stomped into the house. My Mother-in-law was quite visibly shaken as she stumbled to the porch and sat down on the ground. Apparently my Mother had gotten upset at the store, unable to contain her curse ridden tirade she was once again kicked out of a store and asked not to return. This was not the first time such an episode had occurred. I remember entire strip malls which we were not allowed to go to. One such episode began with a faulty balloon. No really, a faulty balloon. My Mother-in-law had heard such stories but had dodged the crazy bullet up until now. She was not prepared for the force at which my Mother's obscenities could fly and with such brutally barbed spikes.

That night I had to tell my Mother that I could no longer allow her to stay at my house. She would have to return home. She cried and begged, said she would "be better." I knew at that point that there was no way I could let this situation get any more out of control than it already was. I was not going to take part in that old dog fight.

I remained in essence her guardian for at least another year but from a safe distance. Not so safe that I didn't get hit with a fair amount of shrapnel but I kept my head down when the blasts went off.

Boundaries. They get so damn hazy in chaos. I had none at first. Putting myself in charge was a 24-hour job. I had to-do lists scrawled on pharmacy receipts, contact numbers saved into my phone with no name attached, past due credit card bills of my own getting mixed up with the credit card bills of my Father's, which I continued to argue over and over with them that he was no longer alive and therefore could not pay the bill. Credit card debt apparently does not die along with the hand that swiped it. I was trying to manage the giant tornado of s--t that is left behind after a suicide while attempting to organize the "party" that my Dad had requested. Yes, his requests were very specific.

I would like my service to be a party with lots of my favorite music played. Tom Waits, John Prine, Pete Huttlinger, Tommy Emmanuel and all others known to those who knew me. Send invitations to all that might be interested with instructions to dress as they would for a backyard BBQ. Have plenty of beer and wine and if anyone wants to toke up, by all means DO, with no reservations or worry.

I did my best. I sent out hundreds of invitations with his exact instructions. I rented a VFW hall and made sure that the bar was stocked and my iPod was filled with his music. The Bose iPod dock came in very handy even with the dead cat aroma still quite pungent.

I clutched it to my chest as I walked into the hall that morning not wanting to let go, not willing to turn it on and hear the strum of Tommy Emmanuel's guitar or the growl of Tom Waits voice. Then it would be official, so very f-----g official. The day went by in a blur of faces and hugs. I tried to hype up the crowd up with drinks and laughs but my efforts fell flat. This was not a party. Most of the food went uneaten. A hundred lonely casseroles lined up at the buffet table, sandwich platters with wilted lettuce, shriveled carrot sticks dipped in warm ranch dressing.

The day before the memorial "party" I went into my art studio and using a bunch of old picture frames and enlarged photos, I created some really nice pieces of artwork to display at the hall, seeing as how the average VFW hall is quite lacking in any sort of ambiance and well, the guests would probably be expecting something to look at besides the faces of other confused guests. One such collage came out quite unexpectedly poignant and remains on my wall to this day. My Father stands in a trolley car, he's wearing a Tom Waits concert shirt and his grey leather sport coat, the one with the hidden magic tricks sewn to the interior which he used to amuse the naive. I miss those corny routines; the disappearing handkerchief, the magic dollar and the good ole' lit cigarette into the fake thumb routine. Oops, I gave it away, sorry Dad.

He looks serious in the picture, solemn. The jacket worn that night because it looked good with the shirt not for the cheap laughs. My Mother says she took the picture, pretty good camera work for a woman with less than 10% of her vision left. It may be the most honest picture I have ever seen of my Father. His classic smile taking a break, his eyes unveiled and letting a little of the darkness sneak out. Most of the time his darkness was camouflaged by humor and charisma.

Camouflaged by humor and charisma...the perfect hiding place for depression. It had been there his whole life, I saw it in his eyes. Most people were too distracted by his charms to notice. Anyone can smile for a camera, he smiled for everyone and spread that s--t like a comedic plague. It was damn hard to be in a bad mood around him, his own pain so deeply embedded in him that it acted like a vacuum, sucking in any surrounding sadness or grief. All of this pain turned into a sort of fuel that kept him going, *how much more can I handle?*

He held on for as long as he could. Until one day he just couldn't hold on anymore.

WHERE IS THE SHAME?

By Julie Wilson

As many of you know, suicide is a part of our life. Really, it's a part of most families in one way or another, but it took a very personal turn in our life in 2008. Today we are inundated with suicide. It's in the paper, on the local news, or online. We see it in movies, TV, it's everywhere! So why is there still so much shame behind that one awful word? How many times have you heard a person say, "I'm ashamed to say I almost thought about taking my own life??

Ashamed?? Shouldn't that word be changed to SAD? It's sad to feel that alone; that overwhelmed with life; that scared to think the only way to end your pain, is to end your life. I, myself, change the way I hear suicide. I am flipping it in my head every time I hear the word "commit" to "died by." After all, for one to "commit" suicide sounds like a crime... what is the punishment for said crime? The only crime is society's ignorance. The mere fact that people can't/won't get help says a lot about us, that as a society we see that person as weak or cowardice for feeling so sad or overwhelmed. When will it be OK to talk about wanting to end one's life without fear? In some instances, if a person even *suggests* they think about suicide, they can be held on a mental health hold against their will! That, in itself, could be a factor as to why most people (especially men) never talk about it. Can you imagine going to the doctor and telling them you think you have a cold, only to be told they have to keep you for your own protection?!

In order for people to be less afraid, there have to be changes in the very basics of suicide and depression. Take the shame out of it. There is no shame in feeling bad. The shame should be on the side of people who, in this day and age, are not educated enough to understand that depression is an illness, not a weakness; and certainly not a sin against God. Depression (*and other mental health illnesses*) is an illness just like any other illness. I can no longer sit by and let people shame me or anyone I love simply because they or I have an illness you cannot see or understand. To say to someone: "snap out of it, you're alive aren't you?" or "Come on, life is not that bad." Really!!!? Would you tell someone with cancer to snap out of it? Wake up people! This is not going away until a cure can be found. Until then, we will continue to see that someone dies by suicide every 16 minutes.

MY SON

By Connie Kennemer

I loved my son."
        Write it on my gravestone—
        Say it in my eulogy.
Speak it simply,
Tell it truly—
I loved my son.

Don't regale songs I've sung
Or tales I've told
Or carols I've crafted.
Only this: I loved my son.
The air is sweet, but silent now—
Just breathe a blessing,
Proclaim the prayer that is eternal,
And needs no amen.
Ponder the holy pause, the *selah;*
The legacy that lives on
For time and eternity:
"I loved my son."

I wrote this while on a family vacation in beautiful Victoria, British Columbia in June of 2005. The inspiration brought more questions than creative satisfaction. Why this? Why now?

Less than six months after this was penned, Todd Michael Kennemer took his own life after a cruel and crushing battle with bipolar disorder, a mental illness that has a 25% suicide rate for young adults. I miss Todd with my every breath and heartbeat, but I rest knowing he is free from the torture chamber his mind had become.

I now understand this puzzling tribute. It is a prophetic whisper from heaven, with only one small change to reflect the present: the air is sweet, but it is not silent. The atmosphere is filled with the voices of a thousand friends, with music, laughter, tears and memories that will enrich all of our lives…until we see God face to face, and our Todd close at hand.

LIFE WITHOUT TODD

By Rex Kennemer

January 10, 2006

Connie and I are Todd's parents. He took his life in Seattle on November 17, 2005. Todd was 25. He had just made new friends at the National Alliance on Mental Illness (NAMI) office, not far from his apartment. He thought it would be good to have a dog like London, the black lab he met there. We heard hope in his voice. He thought it would be good to volunteer there. We heard purpose in his heart. He thought that living alone was not healthy for now, something we had felt for some time. But the answer to that didn't come soon enough.

We've been asked to share how we are coping as parents. Three memorial services in three cities, followed by his graveside service, leave us feeling completely drained and wanting to crawl in a hole ourselves. This is some of my first writing since Todd's death. I'm prone to go back and pick up where I left off in my journaling, the last day I saw my son. He had checked himself into a hospital. One month later, the day he died, the hospital was holding a bed for him. His doctor, his therapist and many friends were looking for him, and yet, he felt completely alone in his illness. Words meant so much to this once sharp mind. Now he could barely answer a simple question, much less express the pain of his mental prison.

Since Todd's diagnosis of bipolar in December 2004, we began to learn what we could about the disease. Now it is shocking to us how little we heard or read about one common outcome: suicide. Now we live under the cloud of two stigmas, mental illness and suicide, stigmas that feed on lack of knowledge. But we're learning how intermingled these two really are. In my simple reasoning, I say, Todd took his life; he died of mental illness. To me, these are two truths held in tension by each other. Did he have a choice? Yes, I guess. But his mental anguish drove him into an unbearable kind of isolation. I'm thankful he is not there any longer. For now, I can't be mad at him. I wish everyone felt this way. I wish I could always feel this way. No doubt, there are days ahead when I'll want to scream at him, Why? I won't expect an audible answer, but I imagine hearing him say to me what I want to say to him: "I did the best I could."

LOSING YOU, MY BIG SISTER...

By Deborah Saenz

Natalie Lynn Gonzales...

On November 2, 2010, little did I know that day would become a living nightmare. The phone call came from my sister's friend at about 3:30pm. The things my sister was saying had scared her. I called my sister and she tried to pretend everything was okay. I knew better. She had already made one attempt on her life. I tried to talk her out of hurting herself, but it was to no avail. I sped to her condo to stop her, but she wasn't there. I searched for her. After being unable to find her, I notified the police. I gave them her picture and they looked up her license plate number. She was listed as a missing person at risk and I was given a case number. I was told finding her would be like "finding a needle in a hay stack." However, I couldn't just sit and do nothing, so on a hunch I started calling hotels. At 10:00pm, I finally found the hotel where my sister had checked in. I called 911 and was met at the hotel. Her car was there! The door was broken down. I tried to go in, but the police wouldn't let me. I fought the police anyway. I wanted to be with my sister! I had to tell her to hold on! I had to tell her not to leave! If my dad had not been there, I would have probably been in handcuffs. I started crying and screaming uncontrollably while my dad held me against the rail. A migraine hit, so I had to regain control. My younger sister came to the hotel. The EMTs worked on my sister for what seemed to be forever. I kept asking what hospital she would be taken to. Then, came the terrible, awful, fateful news, "We're sorry, but all efforts were made..." The words echoed in my head. I couldn't grasp them! She couldn't really be gone. Part of me died that night. How could we tell my mom? I called my aunt and my mom's best friend. My younger sister called our uncle and aunt. We needed support for my mom. We needed support for us! I had to be strong. I was always the calm, level headed sister.

There were people to notify and people to comfort. I saw my dad cry. I had to make the plans, because everyone else was too upset. I had to contact the mortuary and call the cemetery. I called the Deacon and helped to plan her memorial service. I needed to get the obituary written. I also had to find a lawyer since there wasn't a legal will. People were constantly in and out of my mom and dad's house. I spent the next two weeks at their house. There was no time to cry. The PAIN was so intense!!! My heart physically hurt! It was exhausting! Why? What if I had just found her sooner? Why didn't she want help? My God how would our family ever get through this? After two weeks, most people stopped calling and going over to my parent's house. I put a smile on my face and went back to teaching. I did not want hugs or condolences. I wanted to forget and go back to "normal." I functioned at school, but on the way home the emptiness, pain, anger, sadness and guilt hit. All of which, can cause a person to go mad! As the days passed, I did the best I could. Still, I let my class, house and myself go. I isolated myself. I didn't have energy. I had no drive. The PAIN was too intense. I didn't cry. So much ANGER! My heart hurt with every beat. I had constant migraines at school and at home. I felt like life had just taken too much out of me, but I hung on.

I pretended my sister was still here. DENIAL!!! Inner turmoil! I changed the subject when she came up. I didn't let my other sister cry around me. Too much PAIN!!! Too much ANGER!!! I kept dying inside. I knew deep inside my big sister was gone. I felt so alone. I smiled to hide the pain. My body hurt. The migraines continued. My sister was everywhere I looked. I missed her so much! I couldn't stand to think of her. I thought my head would explode! The sun came up, but life was gray. The ANGER!!! The PAIN!!! Going into her condo was torture. Going through her things was so painful. Everything had her smell on it. Passing the hotel was awful. Hearing her voice on my answering machine was unbearable. Flashbacks to that fateful night, Post Traumatic Stress Disorder! The PAIN was too much to handle! Life went to black and white. I adopted her poodles and seeing them each day was another reminder. She was everywhere!

So much ANGER at my sister, God and the world. The whys? The what ifs? It was eating me alive! I didn't cry! Too much going on in my head! Life went on, but I didn't want it to!!! So much PAIN and ANGER inside! It was going to come out. It had to. My anger almost came out on the wrong person. I wanted to hit her. I wanted to hurt her. I wanted to push her down the stairs. I saw myself doing it! I got a ticket going 97 mph! I had to regain control of my life or it

would be the end of me! I had too much to lose. I didn't want my family to suffer any more pain. After five months, I got help. I HAD TO!

I found a great therapist. My sister and I began going to the SOSL support group. Still pain! Still anger! Her birthday came! My family and I went out to dinner. We let balloons go with notes on them for her. I sent her a kiss, too! I didn't cry often. I still had flashbacks to that night. It was still hard to look at her pictures. I smelled her. I felt her presence. She should have been at my son's wedding. My other sister and I raised money for the SOSL Save a Life Walk. Each year our group grows bigger.

As the years passed, I began to understand. I started to remember the good memories. The good days outnumber the bad. I am still seeing a wonderful therapist. I can see what had always been in front of me- an awesome little sister, son, niece and nephew... a loving mom, dad and extended family... so many wonderful friends... an awesome, loving boyfriend... loving/caring coworkers...a beautiful home... a good life! I think about my sister every day, but I can smile for real. My heart will always have a big hole in it that nobody could ever fill. I don't always want to talk about her. It hurts to look at pictures of her. I still don't cry much.

When I think or talk about my sister, my heart hurts and it is hard to breathe. Anxiety! I still have anger issues with my sister and God, but I understand that I am grieving. I understand that it will take an unspecified amount of time and that I need to go through this. Reading about suicide and what survivors have been through has helped. Talking and writing about my feelings and what I went through helped, too. I have reconnected with life, a new way of life. I still can't believe my sister is gone. I will always miss her like crazy. Although there are good and bad days, I know that I am blessed and I will always cherish the good memories with my sister.

Part II
Grief

"*All human life has its seasons and cycles, and no one's personal chaos can be permanent. Winter, after all, gives way to spring and summer, though sometimes when branches stay dark and the earth cracks with ice, one things they will never come, that spring, and that summer, but they do, and always.*"

—*Truman Capote*

LET IT EVOLVE

By Brooke James

Summer, 2013

"Yes" was his last word.

He had been asked if there was anyone he would like them to call.

It was just before four in the morning and his family was sleeping. His wife and children were in their beds and the morning glow of dawn had yet to approach. His little girl had spoken to him on the telephone the evening prior; he hadn't seen her in a few weeks but he would see her tomorrow. She had just returned from a trip to the east coast. She had souvenirs and stories for him. She'd missed him.

But he passed away, and the nurse didn't have time to call us.

***

Throughout the beginning of his illness my father took me to school every morning on his way to work. I was in middle school at the time, shy and unsure and oblivious of all life could deal out. We used to give my friend, Jeni, a ride; she didn't live far from the school so we would pick her up on the way. To be honest, I don't remember *meeting* Jeni, I just remember *knowing* her. She lived in a small crooked house with a long uneven dirt road of a driveway that led up to the pile of tattered old wood and peeling paint. Dust would fly up around the car like an angry sandstorm that guarded the hovel from intruders. Usually, she would wait for us at the end of her driveway. As we drove up her street, I vividly recall her sitting alone on the curb next to the mailbox, drawing circles in the sand with a twig with one hand and cradling her chin with the other until she'd hear our car and look up.

She shared a small room with her sisters, her brothers shared another. I can't recollect anything about the inside of the house other than her room; we never spent time anywhere else. Her room was small, crowded by a bunk bed and a small day bed. There weren't any decorations on the walls. We'd sit on the floor of the room and play cards, picking at sunflower seeds until a pile of husks overflowed off of the paper towel we'd spit them onto. We'd play war and gin and speed and go-fish, and we'd talk about the boys we had crushes on. At school she would eat dry Top Ramen for lunch. She loved to play tether ball and had the ability to talk me into playing with her, despite my hatred of the game. It was too aggressive for me, but it was one of the few places her confidence really shone through. For years, Jeni and I were very close.

We put on a fashion show once after finding a dusty box full of outdated clothes and Halloween costumes. I have a pictorial memory of her walking down our faux runway with a lilac scarf around her head, smiling like a beauty pageant contestant, hands on her hips. When I'm overwhelmed by the anamnesis of the flashes from our friendship, that's the memory I try to focus on.

Eventually my father grew sicker, and was hospitalized. The medical center he dwelled within was over an hour away from his former life, a valiant hospital with a beautiful rose garden. It would, in time, become the backdrop of so many raw memories - bitter because of their details; sweet because I am lucky enough to have the memories at all. The rides to school ended.

Jeni and I began taking the bus - different buses; I lived a bit farther up the boulevard than she did. And the following school year we had different classes, and she and I abruptly grew apart. She began dating boys and I began to withdraw. I'd see her every now and then in the hallways; we'd wave at each other, but we'd keep walking.

By the time we started high school, I had slipped into a leaden depression. My father was gone. To this day I still don't understand how we can grieve so overwhelmingly, despair so completely. How can we, as complex emotional human beings, survive such grief? The anger gave way to the suffering, gave way to the darkness, and I began to think about getting out. I fantasized about being free, about stopping the toxic flashbacks, about ending the paralyzing feeling of permanent loss that had settled in. I fell into the hands of Chopin, Woolf, Camus and Kierkegaard. I met Jim Beam. I started my decent down the slope. To say that I didn't care anymore is a lie. I cared too much.

A month or so before our high school graduation, I ran into Jeni, literally, between classes one day. I'd been drinking the night before and wore thick blackened glasses and looked at the ground when I walked. I bumped right into her.

We smiled upon recognition and exchanged awkward "Oh, heys" before turning to go our separate ways. But then I noticed she looked different. All of the confidence was gone.

"Hey," I said again. "You doing alright?"

It was a second or two before she said "yes," a delayed pause that must have held so much thought and emotion in such a small instant. But she did, and then gave me a weak smile, and kept walking. I accepted it. It was the last thing she ever said to me.

For the next three years, I struggled. I felt like Stevie Smith's *Dead Man*.

I was much further out than you thought / And not waving but drowning / Oh, no no no, it was too cold always / I was much too far out all my life / And not waving but drowning.

I drank, all too much, not with friends at parties but alone in my room. It wasn't until the walls would swirl before I felt okay. The idea of putting everything to a screeching end was always at the forefront of my mind. And I began to think about *how*...

But then I found out. I found out Jeni was gone.

My home town is small and news travels quickly. I'd moved away to go to school, but the information found its way to me nonetheless. It hit me like a punch to the stomach; that feeling of suffocation, of your lungs desperately trying to suck in oxygen as you keel over and time stands still, that moment of feeling like you're never going to breathe again.

I don't know how, and I don't know why. There were rumors about how she did it, but her family kept it quiet. There were rumors about why she did it, and those rumors I believe, but they're not important now. When you really think about it, the *why* is always the same, at the core of it, underneath it all and at the root of it.

I don't mean to say it's not important. What I mean to say is, I can't focus or dwell on the *why* because it is absolutely vital, for my survival, not to. It happened. And no matter how many times I try to turn back time, no matter how many times I try to figure out a way to help her, how many times I replay our last encounter or try to recall any signs I missed, all the ways I might have prevented it, all the ways I felt like it was somehow my fault, like I failed her, as though I had sat back and *let* it happen, regardless of all of that, I can't save her.

But she saved me.

I grieved for Jeni so fiercely, so rapidly. I had hung up the phone upon hearing the news and there were a few moments of deafening silence that hung around me like the stale air of a forgotten tomb. I didn't want to believe it. It couldn't be true. She wouldn't, couldn't. But why couldn't she? Just moments before, *I'd* wanted to.

My heart rose up in my throat and that feeling of suffocation enveloped me once again. How could she have given up? I had held on, why couldn't she? And yet, I realized I wasn't angry at her; I was angry at everyone, everything: at life, at fate, at God. Take your pick. No matter your philosophy, the anger is inescapable. That conviction that you've been wronged breeds the ire and the agony.

And then I became angry with myself. What right had I to grieve like this?

But suddenly, the tears poured out of me like brackish water escaping into the sea. I slid slowly to the floor, back against the wall, and sobbed. I don't know how long I wept, but when my red eyes had finally dried and my hiccups had resided and I'd caught my breath once more, the shadows in my room had grown long as the earth began to turn around the sun. I grew calm, but it was a long while before I was able to stand up again.

I think Jeni saved me from my sorrow. In mourning her, the *process* of my grief was finally able to begin, unhinged from the purgatory of my mind. I miss her, I miss my father, I miss all the others whom I've grown to love only to have lost to the sharp twists of life. But somehow, almost miraculously, when I think of these angels of mine, I am now able to see the beauty a little clearer. The thick haze of the gray fog is lifting, just a little, every day. I think I see and appreciate the beauty and tenderness and compassion around me a little more. And when I start to slip or sink into sadness again, I imagine them happy, free from pain, watching me and smiling. I let the memories of my father's hug bring me comfort, and I let the memory of Jeni in a lilac scarf, grinning and strutting down an imaginary runway, wash over my soul, allowing me to glow once again.

C.S. Lewis once said that the death of a beloved is like an amputation, or like the sky, spread over everything. He also said that sorrow is not a state, but a process. Though all of our individual processes are unique, the sorrow, I think, is universal. Whether you lose your beloved to suicide, sickness, tragedy, or time, you are not alone. The wounds will remain but the sorrow will evolve. Let it evolve. Remember that healing does not equate forgetting. In time, allow yourself to heal and your memories will become sweet, without the bitter.

"We may not have wings growing out of our backs, but healing is the closest thing that will give us that wind against our faces."
—Author C. Joybell C.

BUT YOU PROMISED.

By Jenni Klock Morel

But Joey, you promised you would never do that to mom and dad.
I promised too, but I kept my promise.

I have battled depression on and off since I was 11-years old. My brother battled depression too. Growing up my brother and I used to talk for hours on our back porch. These long talks often went deep into the night, covering all topics, like our thoughts on God, the human condition, human behavior, our family, life in general. Many of my Life 101 lessons came from Joey.

I used to cry a lot because I hurt so badly. It was a raw and tender age, but for me, it was dark, deep, and desperate. At the time I did not yet have close friends to talk to, and my parents were dismissive of my mental health condition, despite their knowledge of my issues, including the crying, the rage, and my family's history of depression and alcoholism.

Joey hurt badly too. Although, it seemed that he wore it better - maybe that he hid it better. He had a positive disposition, a happy-go-lucky attitude, a smile even when his eyes were filled with pain.

He was always ready to help another soul at the drop of a hat. Always willing to step in for another, rarely willing to step up for himself.

He would embrace me in these huge bear hugs, and squeeze me as I cried. Sometimes it made me uncomfortable because he would not let go until the sobbing stopped, sometimes it was hard to breathe through his hugs because he squeezed so tight. I miss those hugs.

With a cigarette dangling from my 12-year-old hand, I remember talking to my big brother about suicide. We answered questions like:

Have you thought about it?

Would you do it?

What would your chosen method be?

Sure it was dark, but our ultimate conclusion was that mom and dad loved us, and that we loved them, and that we'd never do that to our parents. They had given us too much and worked too hard for us to cause them that kind of pain. We didn't want our parents to be the parents who lost a child.

I stood firm in my resolve, even during the darkest times, even when thoughts of suicide swirled through my young mind, then through my 20's mind... and sometimes now my 30's mind.

Joey didn't. Joey died by suicide on April 17, 2009.

Since that day there has been a hole in my heart. Since that day I feel like there is something missing, like I am not a whole person anymore. Have you ever gone through a bad breakup? A soul-wrenching, I-just-lost-a-great-love, kind of breakup? Do you remember that pain in your chest?

I felt that way after Joey died. Sometimes I still feel that pain. It is like my heart is literally broken. My heart actually hurt, every day, for weeks, maybe months - my memories are foggy from that time period. It sometimes felt like my heart wasn't beating right. Like the blood was beating through, but missing its journey through a valve, like it was only halfway beating, halfway working, half alive.

Four years out, most days I am okay. Although, some memories, some triggers, some feelings still bring me to my knees, and I will curl up in a ball on my kitchen floor and sob. Sob for you, sob for your pain, sob for what I've lost, sob for what mom and dad have lost, sob because I live in a world so filled with pain that thousands of people take their own lives each year. Sob because you were too sensitive for the harsh realities of this life. Sob because if I have children, they will never get to meet you, and you'll never get to meet them. Sob because you were not here when I got my license to practice law, because you never met my husband, because you never saw my first house, because we'll never make any new memories together. Sob for the pieces of me that I have lost. Sob because I love you, and I know that you love me, and you're gone. Sob because this wasn't how it was supposed to be, because you promised.

FEELING INVISIBLE

By Connie Kennemer

"Superboy And The Invisible Girl" is a penetrating number from "Next To Normal," the Pulitzer Prize and Tony award-winning hit musical. This lyric portrays a sister who feels she has "disappeared" after the death of a younger sibling. The song highlights some of the complications of sibling loss. Suicide, tragic accident, murder, childhood illness—the specific cause of death varies, but *each* feels "complicated" to the surviving sibling. And somehow the loss of a brother or sister doesn't receive the same sympathy as the parental grief receives. One surviving sister felt a dual loss. She lost a younger brother she adored and "co-parented" *and* she lost the strong parent- image as she became the caregiver and protector for a season. Because of her brother's illness, he got the lion's share of the parents' concern and care. And when the lost sibling suffers from a mental illness, the pain goes even deeper for the survivor. This sister's grief began years before her brother's death. Mental illness is the "silent killer," and she felt its sting before its final bite.

As a surviving sibling, the loss is often perceived as a *second-row* sadness while the parental loss holds the major focus. But who can determine the severity of the heartbreak of losing *any* family member? Sibling loss is both devastating and unique because of the position each child holds in the family dynamic. When a brother or sister is gone, so many critical roles go with them: Ally, defender, hero, roommate, fellow-conspirator, debate partner, friend, foe and playmate...all roles that only siblings share and nurture. Their absence leaves a hole in the surviving sibling's world. An identical twin that lost his brother to suicide intimated that losing him felt like being cut in half and having to pretend he wasn't bleeding. The emotional toll that remaining siblings experience from the loss is confusing and disorienting: "Why him and not me? How could she have left me? Who will help me help our parents now? Will I ever get *unstuck*?" One young man has remained paralyzed since losing his sibling, not able to keep a job or complete his education. He is frozen by the future now that his brother is gone. The casualty list is long.

The surviving sibling often becomes an *only child* with a brush stroke, changing the family structure and adding to an overwhelming loneliness. One sibling confided that she fears becoming her parents' "sole happiness" now that her brother is gone. She battles a sudden and unreasonable fear of flying, knowing that her mom and dad could never recover from another tragic loss. These are the disorienting and burdensome thoughts of a survivor. And who understands? Who really *gets it* but another grieving brother or sister?

I lost a child, not a sibling, but that has stretched my soul to engage with others who experience great loss. I have watched many grieving brothers and sisters suffer in silence—and I am on the lookout for ways to encourage them. Here are a few of my thoughts:

1. Don't assume you "get it" unless you too have lost a sibling.
2. Consider their loss as a *front-row* grief and offer to listen when they want to rage.
3. Some grieving brothers and sisters consider themselves the "add-on" to their parents' sympathy cards. Send them their own.

4. Remember the surviving sibling; they may be feeling *unheard*. Let them know you're interested in *them* and how the loss is impacting them.

5. Remember the lost brother or sister and talk about them. The surviving sibling's greatest fear is forgetting them.

Any family loss is tragic. Sibling loss is especially difficult because the survivor often feels guilty that *he or she* survived. As a friend, you can help just by being available and by lending your shoulder to cry on and your ear to listen. They often need help breaking the silence that their situation has created. Let them know that they matter and that they are not *invisible*.

GRIEVING ALONE TOGETHER

By Connie Kennemer

Rex and I lost our only child seven years ago. Todd Michael Kennemer battled bipolar disorder and lost the fight on November 17, 2005 when he took his own life. That began our trek down the unending, unpredictable Grief Road.

My friend Marilyn said it in a simple sentence: *"Grieving Todd's death is now your full-time job."* And she should know, having lost a daughter in a car accident years before. I soon discovered that this was an occupation that did not come with a training manual; it was strictly "on the job" training. While both Rex and I were crushed by the traumatic loss, that is where the similarities ended. This was surprising and unsettling for us. We were *on our own* even as we grieved the same loss. As parents, we were both devoted to our son; in fact, we were over-the-top *wild* about him. So why were we processing the loss so differently?

Rex's journey was profoundly sad and deeply emotional. Mine was measured and controlled. I found the contrast humiliating. I was Todd's mother and the mother should cry—that would be the expected response. But my tears were dry and Rex's flowed freely. He coped by crying, journaling and staring out the window. I survived by engaging with the prayer team I led, reading voraciously about grief and suicide, and hiding in the stories of others. We were *alone together.*

Rex was mad at God, the only force that could have (should have) prevented this. I was mad at Todd. His choice left our extended families in shock and emotional peril. How could he have just *left the room? What was he THINKING?* And that was the issue: The disease had destroyed his ability to think clearly. Todd's mental agony shouted for relief at any cost, and suicide was the solution he chose.

My contained, controlled grief exploded several months after losing Todd. I had anticipated this shift down the road, but it was still alarming. Curiously, this exchange of roles proved to be healing for us as a couple. Rex and I discovered that we could be both the *comforted* and the *comforter,* depending on what the moment demanded. It was reassuring to see Rex's calm strength kick in when I was crumbling. I was careful to validate him rather than judge him in his times of emotional weakness.

I learned to graciously remove myself from the room when Rex's pain was too intense for me. He had entered the Grief Room at a deep level from the start. This is where he *lived*; I could only *visit.* I became skilled in setting safe boundaries to inch my way into the reality of our loss. Rex had great capacity to fully engage with his emotional pain, unlike his wife. I often teased, commenting that he stored his sorrow in a Mack truck while I could only handle a teaspoonful at a time. We discovered that although our coping methods were individual, they were *our own* and therefore worthy of one another's respect.

These reflections informed the ways we learned to grieve alone but also "side by side":

—We honored one another's grief.

—We acknowledged the wide range between our coping styles and refused to judge them.

—We avoided easy answers and explanations. We knew we were *out of our league* here and that being survivors of suicide didn't make us experts.

—We did not question where Todd's death had taken us as individuals.

—We admitted that being on separate tracks was often lonely and required intentionality on both our parts to stay connected.

And finally, we decided that walking together on separate tracks was better than walking solo. As parents, we affirmed each other for doing the best we could. Regrets, guilt, shame and shattered dreams are just the everyday litter on the Grief Road. Rex and I determined early on to collect what we could along the way and keep traveling *Alone Together.*

SUICIDE:
COULD IT BE HEREDITARY?

By Camille Currier

Thirty-six years ago my brother died by suicide. He was 26 and I was 24. He was very gifted and sensitive. Loved by so many; disliked by no one. He seemed like a normal, funny kid up to the time he "suffered a nervous breakdown." Then, he was diagnosed as paranoid schizophrenic. "What is schizophrenia? What's a nervous breakdown?" I asked my parents. Upon his diagnosis, he was committed to a psychiatric hospital where he underwent shock treatment, psychotherapy and physical exercise programs. He was also heavily medicated. He was never the same up to the time of his 3rd and last attempt to take his life when he succeeded.

On Thanksgiving Day, 2004, I lost my son to suicide. He was 22 and my daughter: 21. My son was very gifted and sensitive. Loved by so many; disliked by no one. He had not been diagnosed with any disease. There was no nervous breakdown. I knew what "schizophrenia" and "nervous breakdown" meant. My son seemed normal up to the day of his death. He did not undergo treatment because there was no diagnosis. In fact, he may not have even known that his silent torment was a disease called depression. If he did, perhaps a fierce stigma kept him from dealing with it properly.

At my son's service that December, an irony existed: As I sat with my mother to my left and my daughter to my Right, two generations of mothers wept the loss of their sons while two generations of sisters wept the loss of their brothers: all within the same blood line. As I experienced the intense guilt of not being able to prevent my son's torment and impending death, I forgot that I had asked my mother not to experience the same guilt when she lost her son. My brother was determined. His decision was his peace. My son's must have been the same.

Kay Redfield Jamison, prolific author of *An Unquiet Mind* and *Night Falls Fast*, writes that "there have been more than thirty family studies of suicide, and almost all of the ones completed in recent years find a greatly elevated rate of suicide and suicidal behaviors in the family members of those who commit suicide and those who make a serious attempt, (*Night Falls Fast*, p.169). But Jamison also counters this statement by stating that "the evidence from family studies is suggestive of a genetic influence on suicide but it is not conclusive," (*Night Falls Fast*, p.170).

Had I been warned more seriously that my children were predisposed to depression and suicide, I would have been more diligent about cautioning them. But without this knowledge, I could not educate them about the impending threat. Today, many years later, a fierce stigma still exists with depression and suicide. It is this that prevents all of us from moving forward to talk more, cope with, and to try to understand this silent epidemic.

My son is now sadly listed in the "In Memoriam" section of his college's obituaries. As of 2005, 7 young people are listed along with him, ages 20-25. Only one has a reason listed for his death: he was killed in Iraq while serving his country. For the other 7 listed, (including my son), I wonder how many met their death by their own hands when shocking statistics indicate that the third cause of death among college students is suicide.

I am now committed to speaking to young adults about suicide. I tell my son's story and inform them about my family's grief. But, most of all, I hope I can educate students about something I knew little about until I had to. So far, my presentations have saved two lives. I do it for my son. But I also do it to deal with my grief and to prevent other mothers and sisters (and all other precious family members) from going through what I have gone through.

I close this article with another quote from Kay Redfield Jamison's: "There are no simple algorithms with which to predict suicide. Certainly no one has found a way to heal the hearts or settle the minds of those left behind in its dreadful wake. **What we do not know kills.**" (*Night Falls Fast*, p.19).

MY DEAR MOTHER

By PauliG

On April 10, 1996 the life of my dear mother, Patricia Ann Gagliardi on earth was over. In the most abrupt way possible, the single most influential woman in my life, could not take another moment of anguish and in a flash, was gone. Although the gory details really do not matter (because the end result is the same) to those surviving such a tragedy, but for quite some time, those details were a focal point of mine. I could not stop finding myself trying to imagine what, if anything, she was thinking about. Mom/Patricia left behind a husband, a daughter, a son-in-law she never met, four sons, a daughter-in-law, two grand-daughters, a great-grand-daughter she never met, a sister, brothers, several brothers- in-law, nieces and nephews, friends and ultimately, left the world with a hole in it.

The sea of emotions were vast and the questions never ending...

- Why?
- What did I do?
- What didn't I do?
- How could this happen?
- What do I do now?
- How will my family respond?

- What will people think?
- Do I use the word suicide?
- Does this mean I might catch this thing?
- Are they certain it was her?

Good Lord, just writing out these questions, brings me back to ground zero and those horrible feelings of helplessness. Looking back, it is like one gigantic panic, anxiety, gut-wrenching-sorrow, attack no one can imagine. Suicide defies human nature.

Oh how I hate not being able to fix this. Lord, what I wouldn't do to make the world right again... I'll never forget my brother showing up at my house sometime near 1:00 am or so... When he told me she was gone, I had no idea who he was talking about. On Good Friday, 1996, she tried to take her life by mashing pills into a glass and drinking from it. She was found by my father the next morning, when he was bringing her coffee and breakfast in bed just as he did so often. An ambulance came. She was rushed to Scripps Hospital in Encinitas. She survived and woke on Easter Sunday. Unbeknownst to me, this was the last day I was with her alive and the day she spoke her last words to me. "What have I done? How did I get here?"

On Monday, through the doctors' recommendations, we moved her to a mental hospital in Encinitas for Psychiatric evaluation and a 72-hour lock down. Not 48-hours later, they allowed her out of her room and video surveillance had her on camera pacing in their parking lot for over two hours. Nurses, security guards and doctors noticed her and did nothing. Mom walked off the premises, down Encinitas Blvd., where she made her way down to the railroad tracks. Enough said!

Even through all of this, when my brother showed up at my house, I had no idea who my brother was talking about. "Who didn't make it," I asked? When he said, "Mom," my knees gave way and I was on the floor making sounds I never heard come from my lips. The anguish was unbearable.

I would have preferred physical torture taking me apart limb by limb versus that sea of emotion. I do not corner the market on pain, but I know there will be no greater pain in my entire life, no matter what plays out. The path of destruction left behind was equally painful. No, nothing would be the same. None of us get out of this world alive, we all die; yet, for me, my Mom was the first person who ever died, and again, nothing will equal that horrific day. That day marks my new measuring stick from which to draw on for everything.

People say such stupid things. No, you don't know how I feel, so stop telling me you do. Stop trying to fix my Hell, it's mine and you bug me! Do this and or do that...ughh! I was mad at God! I was mad at life! I was angry that life was not the way I had painted it in my mind's eye. My boundary lines and my knowing whom to go to and for what, were destroyed.

- Can I survive this?
- Do I want to survive this?
- Why survive this?

This is truly the greatest cluster F--k of all time.

At the time, if I had heard one more person tell me that "time heals," I think I would have gone postal.

I remember my first Survivors of Suicide Loss meeting. I think I walked into and out of the building 20 times. I just knew I would see zombies, vampires, losers, etc. Suicide doesn't happen to great families like ours, or does it? Yes, it does! To my surprise, I was in a room of people just like me and for very similar reasons. To sit there and listen to their stories somehow triggered something in me to survive this ugliness. A ball was out in motion.

Time went by and nothing was healed, until which time I was ready to heal. Eventually, I got tired of being idle and sitting in my great big pile of hurt, anger, fear, etc. I thought about poking my head back out into the world of the living. Life is for the living! I started raising money for Survivors of Suicide Loss San Diego (SOSL) by putting on Golf Tournaments, and I began attending and leading support groups. I later became, and still hold the position if *Chairman of the Board of Directors* for this wonderful charity, SOSL San Diego.

I have thought a lot about something my mother said, and it rings true: "*Pain is inevitable, suffering optional.*"

I miss my mother's kindness. I miss her toughness. I miss her elegance. I miss her smile and her laugh. I miss the nurturing soul she was and how she always knew what to say. I miss her humor. I miss her cooking and the all of the holidays and birthdays. I miss my confidante, and, boy, could she keep a secret (no I'm not telling which ones!). I miss everything about her, even when she needed to be a disciplinarian and with me, this was often. I would not change one thing about my mother, other than her emotional anguish. She was depressed and had been for quite some time, but managing well. Nobody would ever guess what she was dealing with, because beauty, kindness and a myriad of other great qualities she was blessed with, were so obvious and front and center. In fact, her wonderful qualities were so apparent; one would not look past them. What could not be seen was her cancer of the emotions—her emotional battle: her anguish over her demons.

Truthfully, up until she took her own life, I really never gave any of her "stuff" another thought. She was my fabulous mother. Life was grand and we were all busy living the life we were so richly blessed with having. Boy, were we ever humbled.

You know those baby backpacks people wear now? The ones where the baby is in front of the person carrying them and they dangle off the person's chest? I carry my mother's finest moments with me, as if she's in the little satchel strapped to my chest, and I take her everywhere I go and she gets to live through me. I no longer carry the ugliness of April 10, 1996 in my heart.

Yes, we do have a choice as to how we carry on. Yes, time does change things. Yes, life is for the living. I used to get so angry hearing these things from people, because I hadn't arrived there yet. It made me feel guilty to enjoy anything, but now this has changed as well. I want to live! I want to love! I want to laugh! I want to experience life and feel my existence. I want to help others.

My prayer for all survivors is every one of us gets to a place beyond merely surviving, as the only thing more tragic than the loss we have already endured, is losing ourselves to our losses. I cannot bury my head in the sand, I need to live. I need to live for my mother, my family, God, and friends. Most importantly, I need to live for me, because someone out there needs me.

Skipping Steps

By Devon Donohue

It is generally accepted that there are five stages in the grieving process: Denial, anger, bargaining, depression, and acceptance. When my grandfather decided to extinguish his life aided by a shotgun, I went through these stages in a slightly different manner. Once the initial shock faded, I skipped denial and went straight to anger. For me, this was a type of anger that I had never experienced. There was no yelling, shouting, bulging forehead veins, none of the usual physical presentations of anger were present. Instead this anger was a dark, cold fire rooted in the back of my mind, its weight permeating every fiber of my being. Oddly it made me quiet, as if the energy required to fuel my rage left no energy for anything else. I would just sit in place, whiskey in hand, and ruminate in my seething fury.

It was nearly impossible to extract myself from my cyclical cogitation even though I knew it was only destructive. There was just nowhere to direct my thoughts. The phrase *"You selfish bastard, how could you do this?"* ran through my mind constantly. I just couldn't understand how he could commit such a self-indulgent, destructive act. Didn't he know that there were people that loved and cared for him; and a family that needed their grandfather/father in their lives? Why couldn't you think of us? Of course I couldn't see the selfishness in those questions, not in my indignation.

The task of moving past the feeling of abandonment proved to be rather difficult. It wasn't just the fact that my grandfather was dead, it was the sense that my image of him had also been destroyed. He was a huge role model for me, and was someone that I strived to emulate. He was a police chief, sniper, avid hunter and camper. Essentially he had all the traits that a young boy wants to brag about to his friends, and I felt that way through my teens. So when he pulled the trigger, it made me feel like it had all been a lie. He was no longer the tough, burly, man's-man who could move mountains and carry the weight of the world on his shoulders. He became a coward, a man too weak to live his own life, and sought the easiest way out.

The feeling of resentment of losing a childhood idol ebbed after a few months, but the anger remained. I was able to break free of my selfish accusations, and focused more on trying to understand why he did it, what his thought process was like. I read as many research studies, articles, and books as I could, hoping for answers. When none of those gave me the answers I needed, I checked at the bottom of a whiskey bottle...or should I say bottles. While not exactly the most productive coping method, it helped. As time passed, I came to realize that I was simply trying to rush the process, understanding and clarity could just not be forced in this situation. In order to gain some immediate results, I decided to get a tattoo of my grandfather's police badge and rank on my left arm, so I could carry a constant reminder of the positive aspect of his life. Unfortunately it didn't quite work out that way.

When I got the tattoo, I was happy for a few days, but I don't think I was quite ready to make such a visual, permanent tribute to my grandfather. Every morning I would see it in the mirror, and feel a surge of that far too familiar fury. Every time I looked down I could see the bottom of the tattoo peeking out from under my sleeve I felt a twinge of pain before my blood began to boil. The most difficult part of having my tattoo came when people would ask to see it.

"Hey that's a really cool tattoo, what does it mean?"

"Oh, its my grandfathers police badge, I got it when he died."

"I'm sorry to hear that, how did he die?"

"Cancer."

I'm not proud of constantly lying to people, but I was still ashamed of the last decision my grandfather ever made. It also allowed me to avoid the incredibly awkward conversation that would generally follow. It took about a year for me to be able to look at my tattoo and not immediately be plagued with the image of someone I loved with a shotgun barrel in his mouth.

Right around this time I actually began to recognize progress within myself. I was still reading medical and psychiatric journals, studies, and books, and gaining insight into depression and suicide from a clinical standpoint. This helped me the most because I was able to recognize it as a disease rather than selfish abandonment. I had been spending so much time trying to understand what he was feeling, what he was thinking right before he pulled the trigger. I recognized that I would never understand what he was thinking, because the level of darkness, despair, and loneliness are beyond comprehension.

At some point I moved into acceptance, and I'm not sure exactly when it happened. Once I saw a photo of my grandfather, and grinned about a fun day that we had on the shooting range. No twinge of pain, so surge of anger, but reminiscing happily about the time I spent with him. This was a huge moment for me, and gave me new hope that I was going to be ok. While I had come to forgive my grandfather and accept the occurrence of a suicide within my family, I still felt stiff and uncomfortable discussing it with people who were not close friends or family. A memoir by Peter Handke changed this for me. In "A Sorrow Beyond Dreams" Handke explored his relationship with his mother and the emotions created by her intentional overdose on prescription pills. I related to several aspects of his thought process, and it was slightly odd seeing that from an Austrian novelist and playwright. This book happened to be a reading assignment for a literature class that I took in my junior year at the

University of San Diego. I knew very little of the people in my class, but when it came time for a discussion, I raised my hand and spoke. I was stunned to hear the declaration, "Well my grandfather killed himself a few years ago, and I saw quite a bit of myself in these pages." I expected immediate judgment, but instead I was met with interest in my experience, which I was more than happy to share.

What I decided to take from this was the fact that there is no formulaic grieving process that you just simply follow to overcome the loss of a loved one to suicide. My reading had left me with an expectation of how I should be grieving and derailed my potential progress yearning for something that was not happening. The traditional stages of grieving may work for some, but for me I experienced what was necessary, and skipped the steps that were not.

MY VERY SPECIAL SON
JEFF S. HUNT,

BORN JANUARY 14, 1971-OCTOBER 18, 1996

By Linda Hunt

My life changed dramatically on October 18, 1996. My husband and I were packing our suitcases getting ready to leave for Berkeley, CA the following morning to watch our daughter play soccer for Cal Berkeley. The telephone rang late in the evening and it was the Police Department calling to tell us that our son was found dead from a self inflicted gunshot wound. The most unimaginable words that can ever be said to a mother are—"Your child is dead." That shattered my life and put me on a very dark road with no light at the end. I had experienced loss before but nothing could ever prepare me for this. I really thought suicide happened to other people—that it happened to people who had no direction and nothing to look forward to in their life. I didn't know what to do or who to turn to.

My son was a third year dental student at University of Southern California. Scott was extremely bright, graduating from high school on an academic scholarship as well as basketball to several colleges, choosing Brigham Young University, where both of his parents had graduated. We never had to worry about him when he was growing up. He was a self-motivator, maintaining his busy schedule between school work and sports. When he was a senior in college he transferred to the UC System to prepare for medical school. He met a beautiful young woman, whom he fell in love with, who was going to dental school and encouraged him to go to dental school instead of medical school. She had been accepted to Loma Linda University and our son had been accepted to USC. They had a rocky relationship with the distance and their heavy schedules in school. They planned on opening a dental practice together when finishing school. It wasn't until his third year in dental school that we noticed a change in his behavior, personality, etc. He was uncertain about finishing dental school and had other aspirations. We encouraged him into finishing because he was so close to completing is education. As parents, maybe we should have known the signs of depression, his pain, etc. but we didn't.

One of my deep sources of pain and sadness is my inability to vividly convey the essence of my son to those who did not know him. He had such charisma, was so talented, funny and no words can even describe his brilliant smile and laugh. His characteristics, little quirks and his uniqueness were so infectious. He stood out in a crowd, not just because he was 6'6", but he was so good looking and brought people into his conversation. It really bothers me to have him blanketed by stereotypes and dismissed as a suicide statistic and that is one aspect of suicide survival I cannot accept. So, I speak of my son's suicide, to break down the wall of silence and misunderstanding that surrounds this taboo subject.

I spent many months and perhaps years trying to rework my reality in my mind— trying to find answers to questions that had no answers—as though the answers would somehow change the outcome. The "if only's" and "Whys" were with me all the time. I replayed in my mind some of the things that he said that I really didn't hear, not taking it more seriously when he would tell us that he felt like he belonged in a "different time." What did that mean? After his death, I talked with his friends, his professors at USC and anyone that could provide me with any answers. We did find out after his death that he had talked a lot with his girlfriend and another young woman, who happened to be his lab partner at dental school. He was overwhelmed with severe depression and we had no idea just how bad it was. The torment he must have felt. Why didn't his friends tell us? He left us a letter on his computer that helped explain to some degree, what he must have gone through.

I sadly understand those parents that will not publicly admit the cause of death of their child. I remember my first experience when attending a "Loss off Child" group. Initially, going around the room with each of us giving brief information about our child, how they died, etc. When my turn arrived I mentioned Suicide and there was a collective gasp that echoed in my ears. I physically felt alone in the room where I had hoped to receive understanding and help. I then knew this group wasn't for me. I was working at a hospice at that time and some of the counselors told me about Survivors of Suicide Loss and I've been involved with SOSL since that time.

Without this kind of support, I wouldn't have been able to move beyond that first week/month. Being a survivor is a difficult process in many ways of course. After the initial shock when the reality moves in, there is a guilt...parents often feel as if they are responsible because they didn't protect their child and weren't there at the time they were needed. Our son was discouraged about school and wasn't sure he really wanted to be a dentist, but we had no idea that he was feeling that adamant about his future. Were we not wanting to listen? We certainly didn't realize he was this unhappy with his current status. Life seemed to be moving along pretty well for him. His grades were good, he had friends and we talked to him often. What went wrong that we didn't see?

I've learned so much about grief through this horrible experience. Women grieve differently than men and this can become difficult for some marriages. Personalities are at odds and one parent may find it is helpful to talk while the other needs time for silence. Many people, friends and relatives, may want to help but not sure what they can do or how to do it thus causing inappropriate comments. I have found that there are two kinds of grief in suicide, (1) the grief caused by the suicide, (2) knowing that it could have been prevented. Coping with any death is traumatic, suicide compounds the anguish because we're forced to deal with two traumatic events at the same time. The death itself and the fact that it was self inflicted. We grieve for the very person who has taken our loved one's life.

I've learned that Suicide is not so much a deliberate, hostile act, it's when a person feels utter hopeless and despair with all the emotional whirlwinds that make it impossible to find any ray of hope.

"The permanent solution to a temporary problem" My son left a lengthy letter on his laptop describing his unhappiness with life. We had no idea he was that unhappy. His letter started out: "I don't want to die, I just can't take this pain any longer."

I've accepted the positive and the negative:

The positive being: I'm a more compassionate person, greater love of people and more tolerant. This experience has made other problems seem insignificant.

The negative being: I'll never know all the reasons why my son made this decision. The effect that his death has had such an effect on so many people that are left behind is troubling but over time, we've learned to talk more about it, I talk a lot about my son. The suicide of my son transformed me. He was part of my life for 24 years. Nothing made sense to me and I felt very alone and confused. Initially, I blamed my husband, my son's girlfriend and of course myself for not realizing that he was feeling so badly about himself. I didn't understand depression and what it could do to you. I spent a long time trying to find answers to questions and the "If Only's." I talked with his professors, friends, people who lived close to him. I replayed in my mind some of the things he had said that I really didn't hear and take more seriously. His girlfriend said that he was feeling a lot of confusion, loneliness and he talked about it with her. She thought he was just calling "wolf."

I know that the reality of suicide can happen even in the "best of families" and to the best of people. There is a misconception about suicide—that he or she must have come from a family that provided no guidance, love or direction and that the person must have been a loser. That is definitely not true. In most cases, the cause of suicide is severe depression. Most of these people can be treated.

For me, giving back has been an important part of my healing process. Helping others through their most difficult time has provided me with a purpose as we honor our loved ones by helping others.

THOUGHTS FOR THE NEWLY BEREAVED

By Scott Johnson

SOSL Board Member, Facilitator & Webmaster

Keep it simple. We can liken grief to being in the ocean. We only have to keep our nose above water. The salt water will support us and keep us on the surface. If we're caught in a strong current, we ride along and keep our nose above the surface. Eventually, the current will let us go, and then we swim safely. Fighting the current can take us under the surface.

Triggers are reminders that cause an upwelling of feelings. If you can, avoid triggers in the early months. There will be plenty of time to work with any triggers later. It's OK to tell callers, "I'd rather talk about that some other time." It's helpful to avoid restaurants, music, social events, special places and menu items that may trigger us until the first few months have passed and you're more ready to cope with the triggers.

If you can, wait until you're ready to pack up your loved one's belongings and to make other major decisions. Things that evoke pain now may be the same things that help us to connect to our loved one later after the pain lessens. It will lessen.

Find one or two trusted friends or family members who will be willing to serve in the role of gatekeeper for you. With the community and the press, this is the person that everything gets referred to. At work or school, this is the person that all news and condolences get funneled through.

There are many ways to handle the strong feelings that come through. These may include developing a practice like breathing calmly to induce a relaxation response, mediation, yoga, journaling or walking; all with the eventual goal of going through—or being with—the feelings.

It's also important to remember the happy times with the person who died, like special holidays and vacations. These are a rich source of support to counteract our tendency to focus on the last moments of life. Share pictures and tell stories to keep the memories alive. In the home some like to have many photos out, others want fewer or to have them all put away. This is one of the issues that normally will have to be negotiated within the family.

What works for each of us varies. As you move through this please learn to trust your inner sense of what will help you feel supported.

Note: Original Publication can be viewed at:
http://griefed.wordpress.com/resources/thoughts-for-the-newly-bereaved

GRIEF, RESILIENCY, RECOVERY

By Dr. Ruth McKercher

SOSL Board Member and Facilitator

Most of us experience various forms of loss during our lifetime. If you are reading this article you are probably someone who has lost a loved one, friend or acquaintance to suicide. The Harvard Medical Journal describes grief as intense sadness stemming from loss. It is a process that follows bereavement which is defined as the loss or death of someone or something important. Grief is not only the sorrow you feel but also includes such feelings as numbness, anger, guilt, despair, irritability, relief, and anxiety.

Grief affects both our mind and body. The journal reports a surge in ailments such as colds and, even, more serious illness following a loss. Children in particular may process grief by presenting complaints such as headaches, stomachaches, dizziness or racing heart. Grief is a process.

Most of us are familiar with the stages of grief proposed by Elizabeth Kubler-Ross:

- Shock stage: Initial paralysis at hearing the bad news.
- Denial stage: Trying to avoid the inevitable.
- Anger stage: Frustrated outpouring of bottled-up emotion.
- Bargaining stage: Seeking in vain for a way out.
- Depression stage: Final realization of the inevitable.
- Testing stage: Seeking realistic solutions.
- Acceptance stage: Finally finding the way forward.

She proposed that we all follow certain patterns as we process a loss. As you can see from the graph below, we gradually, over time, come to an acceptance of our loss.

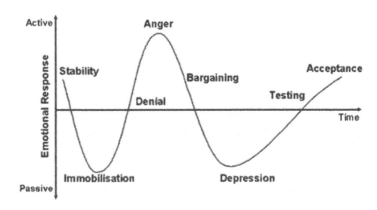

Complicated grief or traumatic grief may follow an untimely, unexpected death such as suicide and a longer healing process may follow such a loss. It is known that the more resiliency a person possesses the faster they will recover from adversity. So what is resiliency? How do I get some?

Resiliency can be described as a process of positive adaptation following an adverse event. The adverse event for most of us was suicide. As reported on Wikipedia, the American Psychological Association suggests ten ways to build resilience:

1. Maintain close relationships with family members, friends and others
2. Avoid seeing crises or stressful events as unbearable problems
3. Accept circumstances that are cannot be changed
4. Develop realistic goals and move towards them.
5. Take decisive actions in adverse situations
6. Look for opportunities of self-discovery after a struggle with loss
7. Develop self-confidence
8. Keep a long term perspective and consider the stressful event in a broader context
9. Maintain a hopeful outlook
10. Take care of mind and body

As we build resiliency we maximize the possibility that we will recover with acceptance, thus, completing the stages of grief. However, for many, recovery is a personal journey, an ongoing process that may involve developing hope, a secure sense of self, supportive relationships, a feeling of empowerment, social inclusion, coping skills and meaning.

THE PARTY

By Connie Kennemer

Todd's Mother

We saw a grief counselor last summer for the first time since losing our son. Rex and I have a very strong support system and a solid faith, both of which explain the fact that we are still breathing some four years later. But as our son Todd's 29th birthday drew near, I felt stuck in my grief. I needed assistance. And I was not disappointed. The counselor we chose was wise, compassionate and at home with the magnitude of our grief. He made a distinction between grieving and mourning, two words I used interchangeably referring to our shadow of the valley of death. Grief, he explained, is internal and private. It is lonely and miserable and lacking in comfort. This described the land I traveled in since losing Todd. In contrast, mourning is what happens externally. It is the lament, the cry of the brokenhearted, the wail that is heard when our sorrow finds its voice. Mourning is the language of tears that both validates and comforts us as we share our laments and our stories. This is grief in the context of community. I breathed deeper as we drove home. Although the details were still unclear, I felt certain that this time on a hot day in July was a new and hopeful connection on this still punishing path. The idea almost an epiphany was born on the way home: Give a PARTY on Todd's birthday.

It sounded a little weird, but Rex jumped on it! The party plan: Connie would invite a circle of friends and Rex would prepare and serve us lunch. But who to invite? Our support circle was large and our house was small. Planning time was short, energy levels even shorter so we agreed on a sampler of the friends who lived in our home the days following Todd's death. They answered our phone, planned his memorial, made airline reservations, drove us to the airport, and reminded us to keep breathing. We included some new friends we've met since starting this journey, friends who fit in our new neighborhood of loss. Like us, they didn't choose the move, it chose them. Todd's birthday balloon was carefully secured within the branches of the tree our neighbor Nancy had planted in his memory. My lovely girlfriends arrived with flowers in hand and smiles on their faces. Rex, always comfortable in a room full of women, was a stunning host!

I realized earlier in the preparation that I had no idea what would happen during the following two hours. But my friends did. Mary started, pulling out a piece of paper and reading what she had penned in the early hours of Todd's 29th birthday. An ovation rolled off her tongue, leaving us speechless and wiping our eyes. Barb shared how the impact of Todd's life has motivated her to get involved in the lives of young people.

Beth took a different turn, risking a confession she needed to make. Our relationship, always close, had become strained in Todd's absence. We seldom talked about him. We talked a lot about her children. It had become too painful for me and I distanced myself for my own protection. Beth told her story in this small circle of friends, some of whom she had just met. She admitted that after a couple of years she wondered when we would get on with our lives. But after a crushing conflict with one of her own adult children that left her wondering if they would ever speak again, it dawned on her: Rex and Connie wake up daily to the painful reality that they will never hear

Todd's voice. Puddles formed in the eyes of my table guests (and host). "I am SO sorry, Connie. Can you forgive me? Will you?" Who would have guessed that a birthday party would be the means of restoring a friendship?

Linda, new to this neighborhood, brought copies of old programs from CYO (Civic Youth Orchestra) with the names of our sons in the list of performers! They undoubtedly weren't strangers. But Linda and I had been until now. We laughed about those Saturday mornings of dropping our boys off at Palomar College and picking them up, three hours later. We could have been carpooling!

Patty teaches an intro-to-computers class at SDSU. At the beginning of every semester she hands out Yellow Ribbon suicide prevention cards that read: Be a Link. Save a Life. She shows a Todd video and encourages conversation. And what did Rex and I say about Todd? Not a word. Our friends said it all. This was the birthday party for Todd that will live in our hearts forever. I am sure there are some who might push back on the distinction between grief and mourning. But for me? I am living and breathing the difference. Sharing grief in the context of community has been both therapeutic and cathartic. There is a psalm that sums it up: *Weeping may remain for a night; but joy comes in the morning.* And sometimes it comes in the mourning.

An Ovation

By Mary K. Jenson

July 30, 2009

I see him as a man, your boy,
dimpled and smiling,
hair spiked out like sparklers.
A face so many mothers could love.

Those funky ear plugs, tattoos, and blue nails.
My conservative, conformist self
whispering, "Why, oh *why*, young people?"
all the while the rebellious fashionista inside me shouts
"Who does your hair?"

They don't like his pockets,
you told me.
And together we marveled
at the attempts of some
to shave off the brilliant facets
of our shining stars
to fit in their round, smooth holes.

How do you do it, I wonder, day after day?
How do you wake up—
no, how do you *get* up—
with such a weight binding you to earth?

Then, I actually imagine him an angel, your boy,
dancing hip hop around your shoulders
like a living halo,
his deft fingers making music in your hair,
joy floating about him like fairy dust,
words of love and hope and "see you soon"
settling gently in your heart.

And it almost makes me want to get a tattoo
just to be in on the fun.

SIBLING LOSS

By Rebecca Engel

David took his life. He left me to be the only child in our family. As the surviving sibling, the challenges have been overwhelming. David's gone, and he chose to leave. I will never have physical or emotional contact with him again on this earth, and that breaks my heart.

David was my closest companion. He was my constant playmate, someone I got in trouble with, someone that knew my little quirks and what made me tick, what made me laugh and what made me cry. I thought he would always be there in my life and that we'd trade childhood memories as we aged. I imagined us growing old together and building new memories along the way. But there will be no new memories, at least in this life.

I remember so many experiences of our childhood, some of them humorous and endearing. My parents will never forget when David and I "went camping" in the back yard, making a tent by tying a rope between two trees and hanging a sheet over it. We convinced our parents it was fine for us to sleep out there all night. That brings a smile to my face. I wish I had more time to build more funny, crazy adventures. My brother won't be around for any family events. He won't be a groomsman in my wedding or help me dedicate my children. He will be absent from the part of my life that still awaits me.

David and I saw things from a similar plane as brother and sister. When this is jerked away from you in a heartbeat, you are lost and disoriented. He was the one I talked to about our future, our plans, our friends. Now I have only questions and a hole in my heart, where David used to be.

This is the first major loss in my family and I am uncertain as to how to walk a road so unfamiliar. Someone gave me counsel that chilled me with its imagery—" *it's like having a limb amputated and still having pain or phantom memories. You know a part of you is gone forever.* "

David's suicide seldom comes up with people I'm not close to. Why was life so hard for him in that brief moment of his decision? I wish I understood, but I don't. Because he was my brother and because I love him, I don't want him to be judged for his actions. Yes, David had his problems—he was a *pain* at times. Don't we all mess up along the way? But we all have something redemptive to offer as well. This is how we want to be remembered—by what our lives contributed. Obviously, life was unbearable for him at the time he made this decision. None of us knew the depth of what he was experiencing. I just know my brother did so many important things in my life and he deserves to be remembered well.

As I wrestle to live with my sibling's death, the path before me seems never-ending. There is grief, sadness, anger, loneliness, sometimes relief, and a variety of other unruly emotions that are a part of this new season of loss. Many of my friends feel I should be finished and moving toward grief recovery. I can promise you, that's not going to happen any time soon. This has changed me forever. Some think that my parents have been more impacted than me. They're mistaken. My folks hurt and mourn, but so do I. My pain and hurt cuts like a knife. Instead of asking about how my parents are holding up, I wish someone would inquire about me personally. I am longing to hear the question—" How are you doing? What is life like now without your brother?"

My brother's death has reoriented the social dynamics of holidays, family gatherings and time with friends. David *is* the "elephant in the room" and probably always will be. And it is at these gatherings that my pain *peaks*. My mind goes into overdrive as I review where he would be seated at the Christmas table. I think of funny or *annoying* comments he would throw into the conversation, just to get a rise out of someone. David will never hear greetings like, "Happy Birthday!" or "Merry Christmas!" again. And when I hear these greetings, they are in the context of the brother who is *not* "in the room." I watch my parents' sadness when others in the family fail to mention his name, as if it's *normal* that he's not here. I miss David so much at times like this. Maybe special days will get easier at some point. Right now, they are almost unbearable. David did you know how much your choice would hurt? Probably not. You would have chosen differently, I am sure of it.

This is a journey I was unprepared for. I am doing what I can to process the season I am in. I am reading books, exploring the Bible, looking for others with similar journeys and unique experiences such as mine. Sometimes this is all too tiring and my mind needs a break from the reality I live with, one that no longer includes my brother. A quote I resonate with on a daily basis: "Through the life span, losing one's sibling to suicide sets up complicated grief. With a loss to suicide, grief is already difficult. By adding the factors relating to sibling loss, we are reminded of the uniqueness of the sibling bond."

David, I am reminded daily of how unique you were and how much you are missed by your sister.

WATCH YOUR MOUTH

By Jenni Klock Morel

Oh, that makes me want to kill myself!" dramatically declares a stranger, or the television, or even, a close friend. My gut wrenches. Literally, I have a physical reaction when I hear these words. It makes me want to stand up and scream:

"Really? REALLY? My brother killed himself. (insert awkward silence) Now... would you care to rephrase?"

Instead I roll my eyes at the stranger, or decide there is less-offensive programming elsewhere, or, if with a friend, I politely smirk and make a mental note to talk to them about my brother so they can better understand how careless, even hurtful, those words are.

Someone actually said these words at my brother's funeral. Yes, you read that right—at a funeral service held for a person, a real human being, who died by suicide, a family member jokingly said those words. I remember sucking in a breath and literally being too shocked to say anything. I'm near certain those words will never carelessly slip out of those lips again - she looked horrified at her own words, I didn't have to step forward with mine.

To be certain, those careless words slipped from my lips a time or two in my youth. But when I was 14 my one of my boyfriend's best friends... one morning he made the 20-mile journey from the suburbs into downtown Detroit. With his hat in one hand, and his skate board in the other, he jumped off the top of a parking structure.

Those words never carelessly slipped from my mouth again.

Two weeks after my 19th birthday my friend Bill died by suicide. It was his third attempt (that I know of). He had tried pills, jumping off a roof, and finally he hung himself. Bill was diagnosed the year prior with Bipolar Disorder. A word of caution to the world—when Bill died he had been "getting better." He had 'found' God and had quit smoking... but if you knew Bill, that wasn't him... Our high school crew piled into planes, trains, and automobiles and made the trip to New Jersey for what would forever be our first funeral for a lost friend.

When I was 27 my brother took a handful, or more, of pills, antidepressants actually, along with a bottle or so of booze. I actually don't have all the details, I'm not sure anyone does. His wife came home to find him... not conscious. He was rushed to the hospital, where he became conscious long enough to tell his wife and my parents that he loved them. He died three weeks later, to the day. I flew "home" to Michigan from California to sit by his bedside... only to return again for a funeral I should not have had to go to until I was well into my elder years. To this day I sometimes still wonder if that 3-weeks of waiting, wondering, praying was better or worse than a more sudden final outcome. Of course, those weeks gave me time to process the idea that my brother might die, but I think in some ways that paralyzed my ability to begin my first steps on this grief journey right away. It also gave me time to pray, and then time to be infinitely disappointed in my version of "God" for years to come.

***

These three people died by suicide. They did not "commit suicide." This is another phrase that makes my gut wrench, my face wince. To commit something is to carry something out, so I guess, this language is technically correct, but it does not sit well with me or much of our survivor community. I prefer the more positive connotation of the word "commit," to commit oneself to a good cause, to good health, to commit oneself to healing.

Watch your mouth, mind your words. Suicide is not a joke.

Holidays, Anniversaries & Other Special Days

By Scott Johnson

Afifter the loss of a loved one, the following holidays and other
special days can be very difficult, for the first few years, and
for some, these days are always difficult.

As a grief practitioner and longtime facilitator of support groups
for Survivors of Suicide Loss, I want to share the following, as
participants in talks on this subject have found the following helpful.

First, know that for many anticipating of the day is often worse
than the day itself. Make sure you do what you need to do, for you.
You do not have to hold holidays at your house, you do not have to
do things for other people even if they "expect" it. You have the right
to take care of you.

Take control of the period of time leading up to the special day
by the following strategy:

1. Plan the day. Know that what you plan is not as
   important as planning itself (planning puts control in
   your hands).
2. Allow flexibility on the day. Planning is more about the
   time leading up to the day, but be open to the flow of
   the day itself.

3. After the day, evaluate. Was what you did that day helpful? Not helpful? What would you do differently?

We can divide up the year into major and minor 'holidays.' Each of ours will be different. Some have major religious holidays, some countries include a 'Thanksgiving Day,' we also have our loved one's birthday and Angel Day, and a few others as major holidays.

Minor holidays might include President's Day, Labor Day or Memorial Day weekend, and such. Consider using the minor holidays as practice for the major days. Practice the three steps above for them as well. Using this strategy you may find a variety of ways that work for you.

I know of one woman, who was very connected to her faith, she found spending the day in a casino worked best for her. We figured the casino was such a distracting environment, and it turned out to be a good choice for her.

Another family I knew lost a child around Christmas time, so for the first few years after their child's death, they went skiing to get out of town.

Consider too that some have found spending time at the cemetery helpful, while others do not. I remember hearing of one family whose young son died. On his birthday they would go around doing every fun things he liked to do: go to his favorite parts of town; eat his favorite food in his favorite restaurants. They made it a celebration of his life.

When two older teens' sole parent died they created their own special day for her. She liked to cook and was also a dancer. They played music they remembered her dancing to, got out her clothes, sprayed her perfume about their home, displayed pictures of her, prepared some of her dishes, and enjoyed one of her meals in her presence.

For some it is helpful to move away from reminders. For others it's helpful to move closer to the memories. While others do some of each. For example, part of the day they go to visit the grave site or cremains and then the other part of the day they go to a movie or dinner.

Try different things to find what works best for you—take care of yourself and do what is best for you.

WAVES

As I sit in the sand and look out at the sea
I'm aware of the grief deep inside of me.
I watch the waves swell as they reach for the shore
My grief starts to rise
It hurts more and more
Then the wave crash down with a thunderous roar
The tears start to flow
I can hold them no more
The tears will not stop
My shoulders, they heave
My body continues to hurt and to grieve
Then gently the calm returns to the sea
And Jesus is sitting right beside me
His arm wraps around me as He draws me near
"I am always beside you", He says
"Do not fear
The ebb and the flow of the sea will continue
The waves will still crash on the shore.
They won't cease
But I'll wash away all your pain and your sorrow
As I flood your heart with my joy and my peace"

Robin Petteys
January, 2007

Part III
Hope

"In the midst of winter, I found there was, within me, an invincible summer."

—Albert Camus

MOVING THROUGH

By Sarah M. Connelly

I remember that day like it was yesterday. It will forever be burned into my mind. When I recall that day I remember exactly where I was standing, what the weather was, who was around me and how my body collapsed when I heard the news. Even today when I relive that day in my mind, my body still reacts as if it is happening all over again. My stomach drops and tears well up in my eyes. I fight back the tears and try to move my mind to a different thought because I have lived that pain every day. But now I am finally at the point where I can move my mind to a different thought. I don't have to feel the pain every day.

Those first two years I couldn't imagine not feeling so much pain. I grieved for my brother with every ounce of my being, every second of everyday. I remember sitting at my first support group meeting. It was probably two weeks or so after my brother died. I will never forget feeling so out of place and having to hold myself in that chair and force myself to listen to all these people. I had nothing in common with these people. How could they know how I feel? How could they laugh or smile or even talk about their loved one? They obviously had no idea how great my pain was or how to help me. I was convinced that we were not going through the same thing. There was no way these people could help me, but for some reason I held myself to that chair until the end of the meeting and then quickly left as soon as it was over. That was 3 1/2 years ago. Now I miss those meetings. I miss the chance to talk about my brother and hear other people talk about their loved ones. I miss talking to other people who know exactly what I am feeling and it is in those meetings that I know that my grief is real and that I am not alone in my pain.

So much has changed in the last three years. I often wonder how I got here when I never thought it was possible. I have changed. I am not the person I was. On March 18, 2004 the Sarah that people knew and the person I thought I was died with my brother. Of course it took me a while to accept this change or to accept the fact that my life is different now. It won't be the way I had thought it would be. I am not the person I thought I would be. The way I see life and the way I live life is different. I think that this happens to all people who suffer a severe trauma. My severe trauma was losing my brother. At first we see the trauma as a horrible accident, an unnatural part of life. It is a curse to suffer such a trauma. Of course I felt that way and I am usually the type of person that can see the bright side to anything. I believe there is always something to learn if you choose to. But I didn't want to apply this theory to my brother's death. I didn't want to find the good in this horrible disaster. What kind of person would find something positive out of her brother's death? I refused to let myself go there, until now.

Once I accepted that my life is forever changed, I had to accept the fact that I will be forever changed. My kids are forever changed, my husband is forever changed. We lived through this terrible event. How can it not change us? I then had to accept that I had to make a new life and I had to re-learn how to live in this new life with this new person (myself). My kids and family had to re-learn how to live with me and I had to re-learn how to be their mom and his wife, because I don't see life the way I used to. Things that used to be so important are now so trivial. I see the bigger picture. I have felt the worst pain and now judge all experiences based on that pain. So, the pain of not getting enough sleep or dealing with some cranky co-worker is nothing compared to the pain I felt when my brother died.

Knowing that kind of pain is a blessing and a curse. The curse is that when I see people taking life for granted and not making the most of every day, I judge them and see how foolish they are being. I have to remind myself that they act that way because they don't know any better. I hear people arguing over the most ridiculous things and I think to myself, "What an idiot, don't they know that at any second their life could be changed forever and they wasted their time arguing about which way to hang the toilet paper."

The blessing is that I now know that I was only living my life half way. I was one of those people arguing about the details of toilet paper. I was one of those people who was waiting for life to happen. I always thought, "One day Dylan and I will reconnect." One day my brother will see what a mess his life is. I'll just wait and see what happens. I won't say anything because I don't want to upset him. I have time. He has time. Now I know differently. I don't wait anymore. The list of things I want to do is being done now. I am painfully aware that my life could change in an instant. I can't afford to waste time on bad relationships, trivial arguments or on living my life for other people. That is who I was before Dylan died. The person I am now gets right to the point and has no patience for wasted time and I see every day as an opportunity. It is a bittersweet blessing because I have to live the rest of my life without my brother and with the curse of knowing what other people don't like to think about. I live with the knowledge that at any moment, the worst thing you could imagine happening, could happen. I will never forget that pain, but I have learned how to use it. I use that pain to remind myself to live my life. I use the pain to remind myself that I am strong and that I can survive. I live the life that my brother can't. Every time I cross something exciting off of my list of life accomplishments, I do it for Dylan. I even force myself to do things that I know he would have done but I was never brave enough to do. While his death has forever scarred me it has also given me the wisdom to live a life that is real and better than the life I was living. His death made me braver.

So when my time comes to exit this world, I will not leave with regrets and what-ifs. I will leave knowing that I tried my best every time and that I gave my all to every situation. I will leave knowing that I told people how I felt and the people I love will never have to question how much I loved them. When I leave, I know that I will have made the most of every moment and I lived the life that I was supposed to and the life that I wish my brother could have lived. I live every day for him.

I haven't "moved on" from his death I have moved through it, and I am finally to a point where I can think about my brother with a smile because I know he is always with me as long as I continue to live the best life I can. That was all he ever wanted. My brother's death taught me all of this and a whole lot more.

Written on November 2, 2008.

SURVIVING SUICIDE

By Lois A. Bloom

For clarification, the use of the word "better" in this article is meant to imply "an improved condition as survivors progress through the healing process."

It always takes me back in time when a survivor asks me, "Does it get better?" I remember asking this question when I first talked to a survivor and my husband (who is a born optimist) also asked it when he called the Survivors After Suicide Program in Los Angeles a few days after our son's suicide in 1982. We were in a state of shock and the full impact of the tragedy had not hit us but we sensed an urgent need for a message of hope.

In the past six years I've talked to more than a hundred survivors in person and on the phone and this is the question I am most often asked. The person really wants to know if his or her overwhelming pain will lessen in the near future. It's an important question. If the response comes from a believable source and is positive it can have a substantial effect on the survivor's recovery.

When my husband and I first went to the Survivor's Program and listened to the various suicide stories from the other survivors I felt a terrible feeling of despair. After the meeting, a few women sensing my struggle came over to me. Facing another mother I managed to ask through my tears, "Does it get better?" Earlier in the evening she shared that she had lost two children to suicide several years before.

"Oh yes," she adamantly replied, "it gets better as time goes on." I recall desperately wanting to trust her words. As my pain got even more severe in the weeks ahead I thought about her a lot. I reflected not only on her words but her as an example. She seemed credible to me after losing two children not that long before.

Surviving suicide loss is much more complicated than experiencing a normal death. Most of us are not prepared for a suicide let alone the complex feelings that go along with it. I know I wasn't. Even though I thought my pain would eventually decrease I had no idea how and when.

When I knowingly began working on my grief work it took tremendous effort and energy. I wasn't ready for the numerous setbacks and ups and downs. Participating in a survivors' support group, where I could listen and talk openly with people who suffered a similar experience was a tremendous help. Sharing with other survivors helped me to not feel so alone and provided much caring support. I could also compare any progress I made with theirs although I soon realized everyone has their own time frame. Reading books about grief, the process and stages, confusion, shock and disbelief, guilt, anger, stigma, etc. helped more than I ever thought it would. As I was processing my grief, I was learning about it. Reading books about suicide helped me to resolve some of the questions I had about the way my son died.

I believe in order to have a successful grief experience one must accept your grief, try to be fully aware of what is happening, take good care of yourself, have the courage to confront the painful issues head-on, talk about them to a compassionate listener (a support group or possibly a therapist) forgive yourself for any guilt you might feel, don't be afraid to ask family and friends for help, give yourself the time you need to heal and find caring support. It's also crucial to occasionally take a break i.e.: take a walk, join an exercise program, listen to music, lunch with a friend, go to a movie, etc.

It's a personal and sometimes lonely journey. It takes much longer than one thinks it will. I constantly had to remind myself that it was okay to mourn but it was not okay to think I would not improve. My life would never be the same but it was not over.

For myself, I found after a year and a half my all-consuming pain had lessened. By the end of two years, my son's suicide was no longer the last thought I had when I went to bed nor was it the first one I had in the morning. Working though my grief was extremely important. I've met survivors who continue to feel awful sorrow for years because they choose to suffer alone keeping their loved one's suicide in their emotional closet.

I will always miss my son but I have been able to find some personal resolution so I could move forward with my life in a positive way.

My message to you is similar to the communication I received some years ago from that kind mother with a few of my words added. I hope it helps you as much as it helped me!

"With much hard work and a hopeful attitude, it does, in time, get better."

READY TO TALK, READY TO STAND

By Jenni Klock Morel

I am ready to stand in my truth: I lost by brother to suicide. Joey died on April 17, 2009, and it is only recently that I am able to even utter those words out loud. I have developed new friendships since then, and strengthened older ones, and yet very few people in my life know that I have lost a brother, let alone that he died by suicide. I know that part of me, up until recently, just was not ready to 'make it real' by talking about it, and another part of me did not want it to reflect poorly on my family, and especially not on my parents. As I lived in silence, what I really needed was to be talking about my loss and seeking support.

In the past few months I have talked more, shared more, and have been met with support, sympathy, and often empathy from those who have also lost a loved one to suicide. It has been a new road in my journey of healing, and I could not be more pleased to finally be here - able to talk, able to stand.

For those who have heard my story and shifted uncomfortably, not knowing what to say, I understand. Death is a difficult topic. Suicide is a very difficult topic. In the course of these conversations about suicide loss simply stating "I'm so sorry for your loss," is appreciated.

As for my brother Joey, I will never know what happened to him that day, what went through his head, how he got to that place to take his own life. Of course I think about it now and again. I know I cannot dwell on the facts that I do not have, the information I do not know, and will never know. I prefer to focus on good memories, thinking of the ways my brother helped me become the person I am today. Joey was eight years my senior, so he always had nuggets of wisdom to share with his little sister. When I was 13-years-old he gave me a copy of the "Celestine Prophecy" by James Redfield. From there we would stay up late into the night discussing spirituality, the meaning of life, the plight of humans on Earth. Looking back, those were heavy topics of discussion for a 13-year-old, yet this is where my spirituality was born, my curiosity for life and its meaning. Joey gave that to me.

When I was 15-years-old I had my drivers' permit. My dad had bought me a 1996 Saturn SL2 for me to drive in circles around our circular driveway before my 16th birthday. I grew up in Michigan, and back then a 15-year-old with a drivers permit could drive with anyone 21-years of age or older. Joey was my go-to person to teach me the ins and outs of driving. This was a scary proposition, as he was quite adept at getting speeding tickets and into minor fender-benders. One day we were driving in our neighborhood and he instructed me to "test out how this baby handles" and to figure out just how quickly my shiny new car could stop. We spent the afternoon driving through the neighborhood slamming on the brakes to see if my car really could "stop on a dime." It might have been slightly misguided, but it turns out that Joey was a good teacher, and from that day on I always knew how to quickly stop my car in an emergency.

I thank my brother for all that he gave to me. For the wisdom, the love, the infinite compassion when I needed a friend. I miss you big brother. I will never forget how you enriched my life, and I hope that I was able to enrich yours too.

To all of you who are mourning the loss of a loved one to suicide, I am sorry for your loss. You are not alone. I believe it is important for all of us to come to a place where we can talk about suicide, to help eradicate social stigma, and to help ourselves along on our journey of healing. I stand in my truth, and I appreciate all those who stand beside me.

Written in October, 2012.

RESILIENCY

Suzanne L. Foster, MA, LMFT

The Free Online Dictionary defines resiliency as: "The physical property of a material that can return to its original shape or position after deformation that does not exceed its elastic limit." Perhaps like a bungee cord or rubber band. Also included in this definition is: "Bouncing back and a return to normal functioning."

I found this definition almost humorous. After the death of my daughter, Shannon, by suicide in 1991, I indeed felt I had been pulled, twisted, folded, spindled, and mutilated, and was "deformed" physically, emotionally, relationally, and even spiritually. I definitely felt my "elastic limit" had been exceeded and that I would never return to normal, or at least not to my original shape. In fact, bouncing back was not even in my vocabulary.

Although those of us who have had major life losses often feel this way, resiliency has a much broader connotation than just "rebounding or springing back." Resiliency is that quality of adapting well and being able to maintain normal functioning when exposed to adverse events. Brad Waters, LCSW ("The Seven Habits of Highly Emotionally Healthy People," *Psychology Today*, May, 2013), states that, "Resilient people do not let adversity define them. They find resilience by moving towards a goal beyond themselves, and transcending pain and grief by perceiving bad times as a temporary state of affairs. Those who master resilience tend to be skilled in preparing for emotional emergencies and adept at accepting what comes at them with flexibility rather than rigidity—*times are tough but I know they will get better.* Resilient people are like bamboo in a hurricane—they bend rather than break. Or, even if they feel like they're broken for a time, there's still a part of them deep inside that knows they won't be broken forever."

In the aftermath of my daughter's death I felt I could heal in a few short months by reading a few books and by going to counseling. I quickly found out that this wasn't true as waves and waves of pain washed over me for months following her death. However, throughout this painful journey I learned that I had inner strength, my faith, and people who cared, and that things would eventually get better.

In the twenty-one years since her death I have counseled many people who have lost loved ones to suicide. I've seen them at all stages of pain and grief and some are more resilient than others. My goal in working with them is to offer them hope that they, too, can heal and find life and joy again. My treatment plan includes helping them find hope, develop resilience, character, and draw on their own strength in four areas—physical, mental/emotional, relational, and spiritual as they walk through their grief journey. I believe that most people have it within themselves to bounce back after adversity—by drawing on their own internal resources and the external resources in the community around them.

Physical:

After a major life loss it's important to take care of yourself physically and have good self-care habits in place. This includes eating the right foods, getting sufficient rest, exercising in moderation, and being careful about the use of alcohol or drugs. Although it is often difficult to do these things well after a loss, those who have these habits already in place have told me that it has been helpful to the healing process.

This was a difficult area for me. I lived alone and found myself wanting to sleep all the time, not eating well, and not exercising. Good self-care is a habit that is difficult for people to develop, particularly busy moms. We tend to do for everyone else and let our own care go. One of the examples I use with clients is the "preparation for flight check list" flight attendants go over before takeoff. I ask them, "When there is a reduction in cabin pressure and the oxygen masks fall down, why are you told to put your own on first before those of your children?" The light bulb goes on and they realize that if they don't care for themselves, they are in no position to care for others.

Mental/Emotional:

Maintaining good psychological health is often more difficult than taking care of ourselves physically. After a suicide loss it's important to take time to relax; rest your mind; set clear boundaries with those who don't understand or say hurtful things in the guise of trying to help; tell yourself the truth and that you do have the strength to get through this; deal with the guilt and other emotions in positive ways; provide a safe environment for yourself; practice self-acceptance; take time to grieve in your own way; and to treat yourself with compassion as you learn to navigate the uncharted waters of grieving a loss by suicide.

I found that reading, listening to music, journaling, and ridding my mind of negative thoughts was most helpful in this area. Telling my story over and over was perhaps the most healing. I also learned to refuse to listen to the negative tapes that wanted to play over and over in my mind, and replaced those negative thoughts with positive ones. This took time.

When I felt I was ready to move on, one of the things that was most helpful to me was finding meaning and purpose in Shannon's death. I was able to do this by focusing on the redemptive aspects – how her death would bring help and hope to others dealing with this kind of loss through my working with survivors, writing, speaking, and counseling.

Relational:

Resilient people tend to surround themselves with other resilient people. They also take proactive steps in their own healing by not isolating and by spending time with safe, supportive people. They also know when to reach out for help, although this can be difficult. Support groups and counseling are two ways to find safe, supportive relationships. It is well documented that people who have positive relationships do better in life.

I knew that living alone, I needed to find safe relationships or it would be too easy for me to isolate. I found these through friends, support groups, and my church. Having a listening ear, and others who "stuck like glue" was vital to my healing.

Spiritual:

I believe there is a spiritual aspect in all of us, and it is important to learn how to express that. A belief in God or some form of a higher power is a large part of the healing process and clinging to "someone" bigger than we are is a key element in healing and moving forward. It helps create safety and provides meaning to something that otherwise seems so painful and senseless. This was vitally important to my healing.

A Slow & Steady Beloved Journey

By Carri Hawkins

It has been 4 years and 11 months since I became a survivor of suicide. Going back to that moment when I was told that my Kevin had taken his own life to this very moment that I write this has truly been one heck of a journey. One that started out with such pain-staking horrible grief to an entirely new outlook on my loss and a whole new meaning and understanding of what life is truly all about.

My path along this journey started with disbelief, a broken heart, depression and lots of guilt. In an effort to ease the pain and in my not knowing how to deal with suicide and/or grief, I stuffed the majority of my feelings and grief into dabbling with drugs and alcohol mixed with a lot of denial. Eventually, this led to major health issues. I lost our home, our business and my dignity; I hit rock bottom. I gave in and gave up!

For me, rock bottom is where my true healing began; although I didn't realize it for some time! The healing was slow yet steady. Today, I have good health and I am in a great place emotionally, physically and spiritually. My journey has taken me from despair to faith to hope to belief to KNOWING!

Although there have been moments on this road that have been extremely hard, I am proud to say that I now know that although I miss Kevin beyond measure, he has taught me so much about myself and about what life is truly all about. I honor Kevin in and through my experience and through my healing.

"Just when the caterpillar thought her world was over, she became a butterfly!"

Thank you Kevin for teaching me not only how to love but how to truly BE loved.

TODD'S WALKING. RIGHT NOW.

By Connie Kennemer

My son, Todd, graduated in 1998 from Rancho Bernardo High. He was an *unusual* kid, earning the title of "Most Unique Senior." Some unusual FYI's: Todd was president of FFA Club (Future Farmers of America) on campus. This was a fictitious club, in that the only thing he knew about farming was that farmers drove John Deere tractors. He had a John Deere hat, so he started the club. He took Home Economics his junior year and was an ace in sewing. Todd took a pair of corduroy jeans and covered the front of the legs with leather, adding a variety of zippers. They were *impressive!* He was concertmaster of RB's orchestra when he was a sophomore. During warm-ups he'd tune the orchestra in his tux and baseball cap, which he removed at the last possible moment. It was enough to make a mother shudder, or shake with giggles. Todd was a master at karaoke and often found an eager crowd to entertain at lunchtime. He had sunflower-yellow hair his senior year and wore the same 2nd hand cowboy shirt day in, day out (until I wrestled it off him to launder).

Todd lived and breathed music. After studying violin for 10 years, he reasoned that guitar was a better match. He made the switch (much to my chagrin) and became quickly proficient on the newly favored instrument. It was pointless to remind him that his years on violin paved the way for the guitar. He would just shrug his shoulders, implying his usual response, "Whatever, Mom. *Whatever.*" I accompanied him on the piano for violin solos throughout his childhood. Now I was enjoying new guitar licks wafting down from his room. Violin or guitar, it was hard to keep a stern countenance when his music filled the atmosphere in our home with such beauty.

Todd loved God and he wasn't afraid to say so. Sometimes he tended to bowl over those who listened, but no one was confused by what they heard: *God loves you, and so do I!* His quirkiness and kindness balanced out his passionate delivery, and his friends *listened* to his life.

That's the Todd you would have met on the campus of RB. Fast-forward 7-years to a young man who had been wounded by the realities of life. Todd experienced serious depression when he lost a best friend in a car accident. This seemed to trigger a sadness and anger in Todd that he couldn't overcome. He quit college, moved home and worked for Starbucks. He was in his element there, loving, serving and entertaining his customers. But something dark had entered the room and Todd couldn't shake it. Looking for his purpose, he joined a mission agency in San Francisco, working with homeless youth. Always a champion of the underdog, Todd would feed these broken kids, loan them his shower and cut their hair if they needed it. They always did.

After a year, he came home, still "lost in translation." His next move was to Seattle with his band friends, hoping for a big break in the city's music scene. That never came, but Todd's depression and anxiety seemed to be picking up steam. In December of 2004, he had a psychotic break that landed him in the mental ward of the county hospital in Seattle. It was there he was diagnosed with bipolar disorder. The Todd we knew and loved was disappearing.

His dad and I didn't know much, but one thing was for certain—the brilliant, funny, creative mind of our son was being shredded by an illness we didn't understand. Mental illness left him confused, afraid and paranoid. Todd followed directions at first. He took medications that left him limp and listless, so he tried others. Self-medicating is common as sufferers try to get out of the pain that haunts them. Todd's thoughts were racing and he couldn't keep up, nor could he quiet them. The *voices* became overwhelming, constant, punishing. *He just couldn't take it.* On November 17, 2005, Todd quit fighting. He took his life at the age of 25.

Rex and I have spent the last 8 years wrestling with a question: *Why?* We knew in our gut there was no answer that would be good enough. As time passed, we found a question we could live with: *What now??* As we began to tell our story, we were introduced to a new neighborhood of individuals who resonated with our pain, but also with the hope that was springing up.

Now Rex and I are giving our lives to see suicide prevented, stigma reduced and survivors supported. Our greatest tribute to Todd has taken shape in the form of a nonprofit organization we launched called CAHM (Community Alliance for Healthy Minds). Our Mission reads:

Community Alliance for Healthy Minds exists to engage the community in raising awareness of and support for mental health issues and suicide prevention, particularly among youth and young adults, through venues of Music, Arts, and Education.

For seven years now we have held an Annual CAHM Forum at a local high school, and each year this forum grows larger and expands in reach. These forums educate, explore, motivate and inspire communities around the themes of mental health and suicide prevention.

Who would have imagined it, that the life and influence of a 1998 RB graduate would just keep growing and multiplying? Who would have guessed that Todd Kennemer's life would *shout out* years after he had *left?* As his mom, I can trace Todd's reflection in one of his favorite Old Testament passages—*"He has shown you, O man, what is good, and what does the Lord require of you? To act justly and to love mercy and to walk humbly with your God."* (Micah 6:8)

Todd's walking. Right now.

To Kyle on his 24th Birthday

I would never have thought that
In 2007
You would be spending
Your birthday in Heaven.
I just can't believe it.
How can it be?
That you were taken away from me.
Oh, how I ache
And I long for your touch.
My grief is so painful.
I miss you so much.
So I'll start this day
As I always do
By asking Jesus to
Go to you.
He'll give you a hug.
He'll kiss your cheek
Each time my mind watches,
My eyes start to weep.
Your mom has a message for you,
He'll say.
She wants you to know that
She loves you today.
God put a hope in my heart
That is true.
In eternity I'll spend every
Birthday with you.

Robin Petteys
January 10, 2007

A MOTHER'S SUICIDE: LETTER TO A NEW SURVIVOR

By Diane M. Conn

I never expected to have anything to do with the word suicide other than to read about it happening out there somewhere, far from me. But one day it came right into my home.

I was seventeen and at college the snowy evening I got a phone call from my father telling me that my mother had died that afternoon in the garage with the car running. She had killed herself and been cremated before I knew she was dead. We didn't have a funeral. That's what the shame and secrecy did years ago. I had no words. I opened my mouth and closed it again, over and over, like a fish trying to breathe. I was beyond devastated.

I was now one of them—people who have a suicide in their family or close to them. The millions of Americans who have lost someone to suicide and crossed that line that separated them from us. It never occurred to me that suicide could happen in a family like ours. But it happens in every kind of family, every hour of every day of every month of every year.

You will never hear the word suicide the same way again. You may not be able to talk to anyone in your family or close to the person who died about it. In time, if we work at it, we thaw and words can come out. Don't censor your feelings, at least to yourself.

There are support groups, web sites, help lines and people who will listen and support you.

Don't worry if you feel sad, angry, numb, fearful, alone, disappointed, judgmental, separate. Anything goes. It is a new road, and even though you are not alone on it, you have to travel it yourself. There are many resources now, such as, people talking about their experiences and sharing hope.

The shock of having my mother die by suicide took a long time to move out of me. How would I grow up without a mother? I replayed conversations, comments, jokes, everything that had to do with my mother over and over in my head. But I couldn't change the ending. I had to learn to have my feelings about it and do what I could to feel better, which included crying, shouting, writing, reading, drawing, therapy. I also learned whom to trust to talk about it, and how to ask for help.

I have come to an acceptance about it. I learned that it was not my fault. Now I also know that many suicides are the result of undiagnosed or untreated depression. Years later, in the way that happens with suicides, I found out that my mother was halfway out of the car when they found her—trying to get out. I had to talk about it all over again, and that's okay. I have made a short film, "After a Suicide," which is on YouTube. I am also producing a full-length documentary on suicide.

There will always be questions. We don't get over it. But for today I have integrated the loss and have a full and peaceful life. Please remember that no matter how it feels, you are not alone with your loss. Reach out so you can get help and work through the loss. You can reclaim your life. It really does get better. You can do this, one day at a time.

THINGS THAT HELP ME...

1. Saying you are sorry for my loss.
2. HUGS.
3. Very few words.
4. Cards, phone messages and e-mails that don't require a quick response—or *any* response.
5. Meals, when I need them. No meals when I don't. The fridge fills up fast when the appetite fades.
6. More hugs.
7. Giving me *generous latitude.* My grief has no timetable; its steps are not sequential. I seldom know when grief will "take me out."
8. Expressing total and painful confusion over what happened. Knowing that you are perplexed makes me feel a little more sane.
9. Cards or notes months after. It's when *your* life goes back to "normal" that I feel alone and my loss forgotten.
10. Say his name often. Out loud. Remind me how much you feel the loss.
11. Remind me of funny things he said; how witty and how gifted he was. Help me not forget him.

THINGS THAT DON'T HELP...

1. Saying that you understand. You may care but you don't understand, unless you have experienced a similar loss.
2. Don't avoid me because you don't know what to say. I already feel peculiar and "distinct". Please make eye contact; if I don't want to talk, you will know it.
3. Don't give me your summation of why this happened. Even if your thoughts have merit, I can't hear them yet. I am still trying to wrap my mind around this.
4. Don't give me pat answers of any kind, especially at the beginning. They feel like a slap in the face—like proverbs that work in other people's lives, not mine.
5. Be sensitive in talking about your children. Don't mention them for a while. I can't relate, and that leaves a pit in my stomach.
6. Don't tell me how lucky I am to have *other* children. My loss would feel just as enormous.
7. Don't talk too much. My pain has damaged my hearing.
8. Don't rush me. This will take as long as it needs to take. Just walk by my side, as my friend.
9. Don't expect me to "get over it." I will *never* get over it.
10. Don't ask me how I am. Ask me how I am **today.** I will try to answer honestly, if you have the time to hear me.
11. Don't tell me I will recover; that time will fill the hole my son's loss left. I have no intention of recovering like my loss was an illness.

By Connie Kennemer
May 2009

Growing Beyond the Grieving

By Bonnie Bear, Executive Director of SOSL

My life was forever changed in a moment. When I arrived at home 10:30 pm on Thursday, August 2002, after driving 2 ½ hours from Los Angeles to San Diego, I pulled into our cul-de-sac and saw 3 police cars in front of our house. My 3 adult children (and countless numbers of family members and friends) came racing out of the house, sobbing, with tears streaming and holding out their arms to embrace me. My friend Keeta and I had been in LA for a book signing and had just left the house that morning thinking that Gordon was doing better, thinking the medication was working at last. He was more talkative, he seemed more hopeful. We were encouraged.

I could not IMAGINE what had happened! "Dad's gone, Dad's gone" is what I heard echoing about me. He's gone? Where is he? It took only a minute or two for them to tell me he was dead. DEAD? How could that be? He was here when I left in the morning and I really thought he was getting better. The shock was overwhelming. No one said how he had ended his life and I didn't ask. In my mind I was running through scenarios....he couldn't asphyxiate in the car as the garage was filled with our son's furniture, we don't have a gun, he wouldn't overdose as he hated taking his medication, the only thing I could think of was that he had cut his wrists and I was picturing this in my mind. Then I learned he had used a rope to hang from the rafters in the garage.

The Medical Examiner asked if I wanted to see him and I did, but only after they had him on the gurney. When they brought him out of the garage onto the driveway he looked at peace and I gave him a long, lingering hug in a vain effort to bring him back to life, to see him open his eyes. I could not accept his death, I could only imagine him vibrant and alive. It took me a long time to accept the fact that he was no longer alive.

I did not want to go to sleep that night because I didn't want to wake up and find Gordon was really gone. How could this be? He was a psychotherapist, he had counseled countless number of people through depression, he was on the Board of Survivors of Suicide Loss, he taught facilitators how to support survivors. And yet I knew that even as an oncologist can die of cancer, so a mental health professional can die of a mental disease. We need to recognize that the brain is an organ that is just as susceptible to disease as is the heart, lungs, pancreas or any other organ. Mental illness is as real as physical illness.

Family and friends surrounded me for days, weeks. The whole family camped out at my house for a week and later on friends came from near and far to stay with me, to comfort me and just to listen.

I struggled with all the questions, the 'whys,' 'what ifs,' 'should have,' 'could have,' until I accepted the fact that I may never know the answers, gradually I learned to live with the questions. And in time, I realized that I wanted to remember Gordon for how he lived and not for how he died. I learned that I had to make the decision to change this devastating loss into something positive in his memory. It is what he would have wanted and to do so was to honor him and keep him alive in my heart.

I soon recognized that recovery is not passive, it takes effort and determination. I found I had to work at moving along on my journey of grief, I had to be proactive. Suicide changes our lives forever and we are a different person because of our loss. Our loss to suicide does not go away, but we can learn to integrate it into our lives. We don't return to life as it was, but we can find a "new normal."

The loss of control I felt at first was frightening, so I knew I had to actively look for ways to take some control in the midst of the aftermath of this devastating loss to suicide. When I returned to work 2-weeks after Gordon's death, I wrote a note to everyone at work, telling them I wanted to talk about Gordon, I implored them to speak often and openly share memories of him. To be silent would be to dishonor him by essentially denying his existence. I hoped my note would preclude the inevitable whispers by openly acknowledging his depression and his decision to end his life. For me, it was the right thing to do as it broke the barriers of silence and allowed them to support me. It gave them a direction for conversation in a situation where most do not know what to say.

I sent my Christmas cards in November (that was a first!) and included a note about Gordon's battle with depression and death by suicide. I didn't want people to be embarrassed by sending a holiday greeting to the two of us, unaware that Gordon had died. And I wanted to talk openly about depression and suicide. The response from friends was overwhelmingly positive and provided me with a deep sense of connection and support.

Another area of support was attending an SOSL group which gave me the assurance that I was not alone. I felt empowered to gain control over the stigma and prejudice that threatened to keep me silent. The group provided information and coping skills from people living in the same community of "survivors." I was with people that understood my loss and the experiences I was facing. I was not alone! That was an amazing blessing.

I began to find a "new normal," I found I could move beyond the abnormal consequences of suicide. I will always carry the loss of Gordon with me and yet I gradually found the anxiety, sadness, depression, pain and the stress moving into the background. I began to focus on helping others and that was a large part of my healing. I became involved with SOSL in September 2004 and have found this community of survivors enormously supportive.

I recognize that suicide is not something that most of us knew anything about before our loss. We may have heard of people dying by suicide, but we never expected it to happen to us. It always happened to someone else, but now we know better. And now it is important to learn more about mental illness and suicide, which will allow us to better relate to our loss. This knowledge will also help us counter the ignorance that brings comments that we may find outrageous and upsetting.

Please remember that we all grieve in our own way. There is no set path or timeline and don't let others set unrealistic expectations for you. We learn from each other, but we don't direct each other on this journey.

Gordon died the day after our 37th wedding anniversary. We had planned to go out to celebrate on the 30th. I will always have the happiest day of my life (8/28/65) followed by the saddest day of my life (8/29/02). But I treasure the 37 years we lived, laughed and loved together. They are priceless memories that cannot be erased by his sudden, untimely death.

You Know You Are Recovering When:

You can laugh and enjoy being with others.

Taking care of yourself is not only ok, but it feels good.

The future is not so frightening.

You can handle "special days" without falling apart.

You want to reach out to others in need or pain.

You now enjoy activities that you had given up after the death of your loved one.

You can share humorous memories without crying.

Your emotional roller coaster is slowing down.

You can actually see your progress.

You skip or forget a ritual such as visiting the cemetery and there is no guilt.

Do not be alarmed if one day you suddenly feel the pangs of grief again and believe that you are slipping back into the valley of grief.

These moments will come when you least expect, but you will be able to handle the situation without panic.

Since the death of your loved, your life will never be what it was and that is reality.

Life has taken a different direction and you will never forget your loss, but the pain is bearable and at times touching the tender memories will not elicit pain at all.

—Anonymous

A NOTE FROM SOSL...

Thank you for reading this book and thank you for listening to our stories. If you want to share your story, or you need someone to talk to, please reach out to us - you can find more information about who we are and how to contact us at:

www.SOSLsd.org

"Tears have a wisdom all their own.

They come when a person has relaxed enough to let go and to work through his sorrow. They are the natural bleeding of an emotional wound, carrying the poison out of the system."

—*F. Alexander Magoun*

In Memory
Forever in Our Hearts

Gordon R. Bear
March 24, 1941 - August 29, 2002
G.R.Bearsy, You challenged us to live life to the fullest and we are all
better because you touched our lives. You remain forever in our hearts.
I love you, Bonnie

Sharon Watson
March 26, 1974 - October 11, 2011
Forever loved and never forgotten.

Todd Michael Kennemer
July 30, 1980 - November 17, 2005

This picture captures the essence of all Todd was:
Engaging, musical humorous, unique, caring, entertaining.
He was loved by all and loved all in return.
Bless you, Todd. You have blessed so many!

Jerry Dale Hawkins
November 11, 1950 - December 28, 2008

Out of the night that covers me,
Black as the pit from pole to pole,
I thank whatever gods may be
For my unconquerable soul.
In the fell clutch of circumstance
I have not winced nor cried aloud.
Under the bludgeonings of chance
My head is bloody, but unbowed.
Beyond this place of wrath and tears
Looms but the Horror of the shade,
And yet the menace of the years
Finds and shall find me unafraid.
It matters not how strait the gate,
How charged with punishments the scroll,
I am the master of my fate:
I am the captain of my soul.

William Ernest Henley

Natalie Lynn Gonzales
May 27, 1964 - November 02, 2010

Your love will be our guide...

My brother, my friend,
Timmy Jack Moore 33

David C. Engel (2/14/83 - 4/10/09)
with his only sister, Rebecca.

I look forward to seeing you in Heaven, my dear brother!
Love you lots Rebecca.

For my brother.....

we live on with a hole in our lives but are comforted knowing that you are watching over us and you are proud of us. All you ever wanted for us was to be happy. Love you forever.

Marcus J. Wilson
November 07, 1981 - June 26, 2008

One less light on earth.

Shannon Foster
&
Sue Foster

1990

Shannon Foster

Shannon

Senior Picture, 1990
Poway High School

Joey-Bloppers & Jenni Bloppers

I keep you with me every day.
You are forever my Big Brother, my confidant,
in many ways, my savior.
I love you forever and ever... Love, Jenni Bloppers